IDENTITY AND JUSTICE

IAN ANGUS

Identity and Justice

UNIVERSITY OF TORONTO PRESS
Toronto Buffalo London

Toronto Buffalo London
www.utppublishing.com
Printed in Canada

ISBN 978-0-8020-9881-8

Printed on acid-free paper

Library and Archives Canada Cataloguing in Publication

Angus, Ian H. (Ian Henderson), 1949–
Identity and justice / Ian Angus.

Includes bibliographical references and index.
ISBN 978-0-8020-9881-8

1. Canada – Politics and government. 2. Canadians, English-speaking. 3. Multiculturalism – Canada. 4. Group identity – Canada. 5. Dependency. I. Title.

FC95.A56 2008 971 C2008-905521-7

University of Toronto Press acknowledges the financial assistance to its publishing program of the Canada Council for the Arts and the Ontario Arts Council.

University of Toronto Press acknowledges the financial support for its publishing activities of the Government of Canada through the Book Publishing Industry Development Program (BPIDP).

This book has been published with the help of a grant from the Canadian Federation for the Humanities and Social Sciences, through the Aid to Scholarly Publications Program, using funds provided by the Social Sciences and Humanities Research Council of Canada.

Contents

Preface

I am very thankful to those who found my previous book on English Canada, *A Border Within: National Identity, Cultural Plurality, and Wilderness*, sufficiently compelling to invite me to make the presentations and extensions that have resulted in this new effort: Claude Couture, Jean-Phillipe Warren, Jules Duchastel, Gilles Bourque, Ed Broadbent, Chantal Mouffe. I would also like to thank those whose continuing encouragement and criticism have helped me articulate my positions more clearly: Myrna Kostash, Robbie Schwarzwald, Jery Zaslove, Peyman Vahabzadeh, Richard Day, and George Rammel for the reference to the *Declaration of the Lillooet Tribe*. I would also like to mention two new interlocutors who appeared as this manuscript was nearing completion: Johannes Maerk and Samir Gandesha. My gratitude is extended to Andrew Bingham for the detailed research assistance that he undertook on the manuscript in its penultimate version. Contrary to almost all my previous experience in this matter, the critical responses by the University of Toronto Press reviewers were very helpful. I am considerably in the debt of my editor at the Press, Len Husband, for the competence and care with which he handled the whole process. The institutional support of the Social Sciences and Humanities Council, through grant number 410-2005-0516, has been indispensable.

IDENTITY AND JUSTICE

If I'd known the end would end in laughter,
Still I'd tell my daughter that it doesn't matter.

Phil Ochs

1 Introduction

We live in a difficult time. A technological system organized by a market economy rules the world triumphant; local cultures and communities are subordinated and extinguished except to the extent that they become consumer fodder for this very system. No wonder that contemporary philosophy strives to articulate a genuine concept of difference as a remedy for the indifference or despair that confront those who cannot lose themselves in consumer ecstasy. If the technological regime can be repoliticized – and thereby mitigated, subordinated, or replaced – such politicization will need to draw its resources from the survivals and extensions of the local cultures which provide the roots of difference. In a time of crisis one must look both backward and forward to rescue the specificity of the socio-cultural formation from contemporary amnesia and push that formation to transform itself to address its new tasks.

Canada has been a dependency of three empires: French, British, and American. Economic, social, and cultural development in a dependency, even a 'first-world' dependency, is structured by its relation to a centre from which the dominant priorities of its existence flow. From the Paris fashion that spurred the fur trade to Washington's post-9/11 security priorities that have restructured the port of Vancouver, the demands of the centre have structured the development of the periphery. If one wants to understand a country like Canada, one has to begin from the centre–periphery relation intrinsic to an empire. This fact was recognized by Harold Innis in his staple theory of Canadian economic development: 'The economic history of Canada has been dominated by the discrepancy between the centre and the margin of Western civilization. Energy has been directed toward the exploitation of staple products and the tendency has been cumulative. The raw material supplied to the mother country stimulated manufactures of the finished product and also of the products which were in demand in the colony ... The general tendencies in the industrial areas of western civilization, especially in the United States and Great Britain, have a pronounced effect on Canada's export of staples.'[1] However, while dependency is rooted in economic relations, it is not confined to them. In the first place, the settler population requires and demands the products of the imperial centre such that there is an early interchange of finished goods for staple resources. Beyond this, cultural ties to the centre structure the entire way of life in the periphery.

To think of the development of Canada through the relations of dependency established by empire means, first and foremost, that space is a primary factor. Centre and periphery are linked by a distance. It is the traversal of space that distinguishes the development of modern capitalism in a dependency.[2] While dependent development certainly has a history, the spatial relations of centre–periphery are more significant. Indeed, such spatial relations connect and link social formations that would be seen as belonging to different historical epochs in a European model. The native economy of the fur hunt was linked to Paris fashion in a spatial relationship such that a so-called primitive economy was linked to advanced, elite consumption. This is not a single example but the dominant structuring fact. External, space-based development implies the encounter of the most modern tendency with an archaic, ahistorical one. Canadian culture still exemplifies this polarity.

Space must be traversed. It is precisely such traversal that accomplishes the linkage. Space must be understood, consequently, not as an *a priori* structure of experience but as a lived experience of traversal in the first place by the human body and secondarily through the technological means that expand and transform the capacities of the human body. Transportation is the first fact of centre–periphery relations. Runners-of-the-woods, canoes, ships, steam engines, railways: through these technologies the history of a dependency can be written as the transformation of undifferentiated space into a relation between places. No wonder that technology has been a major preoccupation of Canadian thought. Transportation has to a large extent now been succeeded by communication such that the traversal of distances can be accomplished by messages without bodies.

The dominant flow of such messages is from centre to periphery. The periphery is engaged in a constant struggle to express itself, a struggle made necessary by the amassing of historical and archival weight at the centre while constantly restructuring the periphery to cater to the needs of the centre in the present moment. The periphery archives itself with difficulty and forgets its own history, which must be continually rediscovered and communicated against the dominant flows of information.

But, also, despite the assumptions of empire, the colony does not just repeat imperial dynamics. Innovation often occurs at the periphery.[3] Such innovation may fare badly given the historical weight of the centre, but it proposes a unique polarity of archaic experience and spatially induced contemporaneity. To think from the periphery, to commit oneself to the articulation of the experience of a dependency, means to struggle against the assumption that such experience is merely the footnote to a longer, more established, history. This assumption relegates our experience to being at most a particular content for forms of thought previously developed elsewhere. Indeed, this notion that 'reality is elsewhere' is a defining cultural condition. No wonder there is a permanent identity crisis. An assumption concerning the relation between universal and particular underlies this condition. Universal schemes and structures of experience are elaborated elsewhere – the great narratives of Athens and Jerusalem, heroic modernity, or disaffected postmodernity – while, at most, we make small corrections and additions based upon the particulars of our lives. To think from the periphery requires that one reverse this assumption, perhaps escape it, in order to propose not only corrective particulars but universal models. Our task: to see Europe as a particular case of our story; to write a myth not propose another character for a tame dialectic. If this tension between archaic experience and spatially induced contemporaneity is Canada's instituting polarity, it signifies a lack if it is not taken up into politics and philosophy.

The procedure for an inquiry such as this is called 'immanent criticism.' It is critical insofar as it suggests that the instituting cultural experience has not yet found adequate philosophical articulation. This criticism is immanent insofar as it situates itself within the cultural experience itself. It does not criticize from on high but with reference to the standards and achievements within the already established tradition of thought, though arguing that they are not yet adequately conceptualized. In a situation of peripheral thought, which has difficulty being recognized even within the culture that it expresses, immanent criticism must begin by recovering this tradition of thought. Such a recovery allows one to place this tradition in relation to the cultural experience that it articulates. It can then argue that this articulation is inadequate in some form, does not sufficiently carry through the project in which it is imbedded. On this basis, other conceptualizations can be risked and new universalizations assayed. Immanent critique has these three components in tight relation: recovery, critique, and proposal.

The development and utilization of the concept of empire in English-Canadian social and political thought due to its origin in a dependent economy and nation has throughout its existence, even in conservative versions, contested the imperial assumptions of social and political thought in the United States and other centres. This is not meant as special pleading nor as the adoption of a victim status. Moreover, it does not imply that Canada is in the same position as the most exploited nations of the world. Rather, it suggests that Canada proposes to its social and political thinkers an issue with both ethical and theoretical dimensions which, when thoroughly taken up, requires a critique of centralizing assumptions in international, or imperial, thought.

Critique of homogenizing assumptions must be matched in some fashion by a defence of diversity or, more accurately, an account of the relation between identity and diversity. The common origin of Canada and the United States in the English political tradition, combined with the difference in the manner in which each achieved a break with the British Empire, provides the conventional terms in which the relation between community and plurality has been understood. The significance of the American revolutionary break, under the influence of eighteenth-century political ideas of natural right, and the consequent influence that this revolution has had on all new-world nations, has meant that Canadian political culture has often been articulated in contrast to the pervasive individualism and a-historism of the United States.

It has been commonplace to describe the different character of Canadian identity from the United States with reference to the greater communitarian component of Canadian political culture. Whether this communitarianism is attributed to the influence of a non-revolutionary political tradition, Loyalism, a harsh winter climate, or French–English accommodation, it is widely accepted that 'America reflects the influence of its classically liberal, Whig, individualistic, anti-statist, populist, ideological origins. Canada ... can still be seen as Tory-mercantilist, group-oriented, statist, deferential to authority – a "socialist monarchy," to use Robertson Davies' phrase.'[4] Of course it is not quite this simple. As Robin Mathews has pointed out, the ideological character of the United States exists within Canada as one element of the political culture.[5] No doubt, one could find communitarian elements within the United States. However, the specificity of a culture cannot be defined by looking for elements within it that are irreducibly unique. Rather, a culture is constituted by a distinctive relation between its contents. It is not contents that are unique – identical contents enter as outside influences and often span cultures – but the pattern of their relationship. Culture is a pattern that draws each new influence into the historically constituted pattern such that the contents hang together, and belong together, in a distinctive form. Elements from outside enter into and alter that pattern without the pattern losing its specificity and distinctiveness. Thus, one way to elucidate a cultural pattern is to articulate the resonances that formative historical experiences have to philosophical expressions, resonances which shift when they enter into a different cultural pattern.

The communitarian emphasis has been matched by a particular manner of publicly representing cultural diversity. Probably because of a weak national identity, due to its bilingual and multicultural history, Canadian culture has tended to assume that there is no one overarching identity or community that effectively could subsume the plurality of communities. Thus, multicultural policy, everyday practices, and philosophical articulations tend not only to have a communitarian bias but also to assume a plurality of relevant communities. Of course, we have been reminded by novelists and empirical sociologists that the United States has never been in actual fact the melting pot that its ideology promoted. The difference can be more precisely stated in terms of the public representations of cultural diversity that form the political culture and reside in institutions. In the United States the substantive ethical commitments of communities to a way of life tend to be barred from public life and thought, whereas in Canada they rather become the content of a common political culture. In the United States a supposedly a-cultural proceduralism dominates public life, whereas dynamic cultural communities are regarded as the private concern of individuals. Thus, Leslie Armour notes that 'what we have in common cannot be expressed through a single community ... this pluralism is related to our communitarianism.'[6] This particular mixture of identity and diversity has been much debated politically, but it is from a comparative viewpoint the core feature of Canadian political culture around which debates have swirled.

The recovery of this tradition of conceptualizing identity and diversity in the present text is structured by its central argument that imperial assumptions have dominated its conceptualization and the search for an alternative manner to understand the relation between different cultures. My concern is not primarily to document this history but rather to show that empire has constructed the line by which a culture has been rejected for its ethic of inhabitation or accepted in a domesticated form as an 'internal diversity' to the extent that it has abandoned its claim to sovereignty. The same problem recurs with regard to internal diversity, where a 'minority bar' is established to the extent that a cultural identity cedes its claim to participate in defining the rules of interaction between communities. The aim of this inquiry is thus to propose concepts that do not rule particular communities from on high but capture the immersion of a universalization in the particularities that motivate its expression. It aims at a post-colonial, that is to say, post-imperial, philosophy.

It is the construction of Canada within an imperial history that proposes the ethical and theoretical issue of the critique of empire to its thinkers. But I do not want to suggest that this issue is unique to Canada as such. It is unique only in the history and theoretic form in which the issue is taken up. Mexican philosopher Leopoldo Zea explained it this way: 'Problems like the ones Latin American philosophy raises about its identity seem only parochial, that is regional, and because of that limited to a relative point of view proper to a concrete man, and thus, alien to what is truly universal.'[7] Issues in dependent regions, whose articulation must pass through the structuring and publication centres of empire, are treated as 'cases,' whereas issues of human universality can be treated directly if one resides at the centre, that is to say, shares the assumptions that underpin empire. These assumptions cannot be simply dropped at will but require a critical interrogation. It is with regard to this critical interrogation that dependency has a privileged moral and theoretical status.

To this extent, the claim for the critique of empire that I am making for Canada could also be redeemed in Latin America or other dependencies. The point is that a new global critical discourse must go through the particularities of place to forge a universalizing dialogue. Addressing this issue does not require a denial of universality in favour of an assertion of the plurality of empirical contexts. Universal concepts and claims are unavoidable in any theoretical discourse. The point is that such unavoidable universal claims often render relations of dependency invisible when they are articulated from the centre and uncritically imported into different situations. The predominance of imperial centres in the propagation of ideas, even critical ideas, is central to this circumstance. An adequate critique of empire requires a concept of universalization that would not go directly from imperial instance to theoretical universality but from dependent locality, through critique of empire, into dialogue with other localities, and toward a new, yet-to-be-articulated, universality.[8] The moral and theoretical implication of dependency consists in a critique of centrism. A centrism consists in the subsumption of diverse experiences and contents under an explanatory scheme that is presupposed as universal, although it incorporates elements that arose in a particular history. Therefore, a return to concrete and particular experiences does not negate universality, but opens the possibility that a genuine universality might emerge through the displacement of centrisms. Critique of empire without an acknowledgment of dependency – that is to say, a critique of the ethical and theoretical assumptions inherent in centrism – would remain an imperial critique.

I do not mean to suggest that Canada is itself without an internal hegemonic structure. To a large extent the Ottawa-Toronto-Montreal axis is a hegemonic centre within Canada. Regionalism derives from the resource extraction on which economic development was based. The linguistic and cultural duality between French and English Canada betrays a difficult history. The relation between peoples and cultures deriving from Europe and First Nations is perhaps only beginning to be addressed with sufficient energy and seriousness. Certainly, empire is neither a problem with a single plane of analysis nor a single solution. There are many axes of dependency and forms of marginalization. Each one must be taken to task in the terms appropriate to the constitution of the dependency itself in the context of what can be called a 'plurality of dependencies' in a manner that can aid our various communities in designing local alternatives.

It is for this reason that I use as examples various communities, such as ethno-cultural communities within English Canada, Métis, First Nations, in an undifferentiated way, as it were. It is not that there are no important differences between these communities. It is rather that such differences are based upon different modes of inhabitation but have been historically incorporated into Canada (to the extent that they have been incorporated) by the imperial force that needs to be radically held up to critique. Such communities are not naturally or essentially different, as it were, but are different insofar as their identity has been structured within the field of identities organized by empire, and then the nations-state. In order to uncover the mode of operation of this structuring force, it is necessary not to presuppose quasi-natural differences between cultural identities at the outset. This starting point can only be fully justified by the entire text, of course, in which it is argued that the in/out of empire is structured by the abandonment of the claim to self-rule, and that the minority bar is a further resignation to rule from the centre. What makes the difference between cultural identities is the extent to which their modes of inhabitation have resisted the rule of empire, the force of empire to make the rules. The conceptual proposal of the text is that a phenomenology of locality provides the ground for a thoroughly tenacious critique of the false universality of supposedly unbiased, because historically efficacious, rules.

All real thinking requires an intense relationship between particular and universal. To the extent that empire impedes this relationship for those at the periphery, it requires that the centre–periphery relationship be brought into thought and addressed practically by designing new forms of communication. Critique of empire implies a critique of this division, that is to say, a critique of the merely purported universality of centres and an openness to the universalizing aspects of the peripheral experience. The practice of critique is thus a starting point in performing an intense relationship between particular and universalization. Such a critical practice teleologically implies a non-centric, or anti-centric, or post-centric, form of thought. The practice of critique implies an involvement with that which is criticized. I cannot investigate other identities in the Canadian nations-state – or embroiled with it but perhaps not *in* it, like the First Nations – with the same understanding of lived history and emotional attachment as that of English Canada, and, indeed, this is the only identity of the Canadian nations-state from which I can write as a participant, one for whom its destiny is also my own. This does not mean that one should never speak of others – as one must, of course – or that external perspectives are never relevant, but rather that genuine critique is, in the first place, self-critique. Self-critique presupposes a particular identity and a participation in that identity from which one begins to reflect. I admit to a suspicion of any discussion of identity that is not reflexive in this sense, that is not about one's own identity, since it would seem to slide into a classification, and perhaps even demonization, of others which is eminently to be avoided. But it is important to emphasize, especially in these times of retreat into supposedly fixed and fundamental identities, that such a local beginning for reflection is the necessary point of access to human universality not its negation. To this extent, a philosophy based in the experience of English Canada is not merely parochial but pertains to the contribution it might make to a genuine form of human universality.

Thinking about issues of public importance cannot remain satisfied with the disciplinary separations that mark most investigation situated in the university. Also, the university itself is no longer an institution apart but has become the social nexus of the active intellect, most often in relation to the corporate forces that dominate the economy or the bureaucratic ones that dominate the state. In this situation philosophy is drawn away from disciplinary specialization closer to its eighteenth-century meaning as the deepest level of reflection on any subject matter whatsoever and its Greek meaning as a way of life: a way of life that strives to think the whole in a time of specialization. Understood in this way, the separate compartments into which inquiry may be locked are less important than its depth, which will shed light on all such compartments. The conception of philosophy operative in this text is that of an inquiry into the depths of a specific way of life.

Such philosophical activity operates within the culture of which it is a part. It is not self-enclosed but articulates and criticizes the culture in which it operates. To this extent, it must take seriously the various debates into which it enters – not merely adjudicate them from on high, but enter into the contributions that other interventions, disciplinary or not, make to the illumination of a culture. Thus, while the current text attempts to construct an English-Canadian philosophy, it is equally concerned with the political thought and cultural politics that may be grounded in that philosophy. The tension between locality and universalization which form these implications is not pushed to its philosophical fundamentals here. The aim is to clarify the character and destiny of English Canada in the present moment. Its success or failure would not be measured solely by its internal coherence and validity but equally by its articulation of this moment of a culture. Despite the commitment to philosophy which drives it, it is not a book primarily for philosophers but for a public which still expects something from philosophy.

My unfolding argument in this text is that the secret of English Canada is the unofficial dream of self-rule at the periphery that unfolds in tandem with the critique of empire. It is kept secret through the perpetuation of the lie that the empire, then the nations-state, sets the neutral rules whereby its parts interact. The tendency of official culture is to cover up its opposite in a land-based ethic, to substitute historical continuity for the break represented through inhabitation of the land. The task for critical interpretation of English-Canadian culture is the development of a philosophy of independent parts through a conception of universality that does not subsume parts by giving them the rule, but subordinates the rule itself to a negotiation between parts. The point of using the term 'English Canada' here is not to deny similar claims that might be made from French Canada or First Nations, but to emphasize the specificity of the intellectual tradition upon which my argument rests and which I seek to extend. To the extent that different traditions legitimate comparable claims, an emergent universalization gains plausibility and strength; we may thus begin to speak genuinely to each other.

The three following chapters seek to redeem, at least partially and initially, the demand that I have made of English-Canadian philosophy in this introduction. The next chapter attempts to substantiate the relation between particularity and universalization within this tradition in both critical and constructive modes through a phenomenology of locality. Chapter three redefines the critique of empire in order to show the limitation imposed upon particularities when they are brought under its hegemony. Chapter four sketches the basis of a principle of association that respects particularities, localities, and yet coordinates their claims to universalization.

It is characteristic of philosophical thinking that its expression contains a logic in which the *grounds* of the thinking precede its specific implications and instantiations. This leads to a certain difficulty in the beginning which is, in the best cases, redeemed by the end. Some readers may therefore find it congenial to begin with the later chapters and to turn to the next chapter afterward. The linearity of reading in any case conceals a logic of simultaneous presence.

2 Locality and Universalization

If English Canada is haunted by its constitution by empire, its social and political thought is no less constituted by a critique of imperial assumptions. This is expressed philosophically as the suspicion that established universals hide, through their very universality, the suppression of particularities through which they were constituted. Insofar as universals emerge by suppressing particularities, they contain a falseness that opens the possibility of critique. In its turn, such critique implies an anticipation of further, perhaps future, universals. Such implication is not finished but underway – a process that I distinguish by the term 'universalization.' Thus, a defence of particularity is woven into the fabric of the culture and thought of English Canada. Indeed, it may be that this is its distinctive feature. However, I will argue, English-Canadian social and political thought has been stalled, perhaps for necessary historical reasons, at the first step of defence of particularity and has not pushed further from a critique of empire toward a post-colonial thinking. I want to recall this defence of particularity, and the discourse of the distinctiveness of English Canada which it justifies, in order to pursue its trajectory toward a phenomenology of locality which can ground a post-centric, post-colonial philosophy.

A Discourse of Distinctiveness

Here, I want to circumscribe the 'discourse' of the cultural identity of English Canada, not to discuss the many issues involved in the cultural identity of English Canada. That is to say, I want to show the main lineaments that made it possible to discuss the cultural identity as such and by what parameters such a discussion is limited. Because a cultural identity is not a natural fact, it comes into existence in tandem with some awareness of its existence. This perceived existence is not unidimensional or commanding, certainly in modern societies where there is some form of civil society distinct from the state, but rather constructs a certain 'space' which allows for disagreements and debates. This space for disagreement is not simply random, but structured in a way which also defines the limit of the discourse, the point at which it is stretched to such an extent that it either disappears or is altered into something entirely different. I will approach a definition of this discourse through an analysis of the main theses about the specific and distinct cultural identity of English Canada during the period of cultural nationalism.

I think that it can, without too great a simplification, be asserted that there are four main theses that pertain to the specific and distinct cultural identity of English Canada. These are theses oriented to accounting for the historical cultural formation primarily with regard to its economic, social, and political dimensions. These four theses are known as dependency political economy, the Red Tory, the vertical mosaic, and that of communication. I will outline each in turn.

Dependency political economy is mainly associated with the work of Harold Innis. It pointed out that Canadian political economy was strongly marked by two factors that are either absent or much less important in other countries, especially those in which most economic theory is developed: the imperial connection and resource extraction. Canada has been a colony of the successive empires of France, Britain, and the United States. In Innis's words, 'To an important extent the emphasis has been on the development of an east-west system with particular reference to exports of wheat and other agricultural products to Great Britain and Europe. However, since the turn of the century, the United States has had an increasing influence on this structure ... American imperialism has replaced and exploited British imperialism.'[1] Economic development has thus been not primarily for national purposes but for the wealth and power of the empire. It consisted in extraction of resources, their export in raw fashion to the imperial centre, and the import of manufactured goods from the centre. This means that the main relations of power are between the centre and the periphery. It has also had the consequence that a strong central state oversaw development and provided its necessary infrastructure (especially canals, roads, railways, telecommunications, and so forth). The different regions of Canada are marked by the different resources extracted and the infrastructure that accommodated extraction. A strong central state thus took on the additional role of articulating a national policy that pulled the regions together under the dominant interests of central Canada. The national state was thus a key factor in the very existence of Canada and its capacity to resist the regionalizing pull of integration into the larger political economy of the United States.

The Red Tory thesis was developed by Gad Horowitz in his analysis of Canadian labour-socialist politics and the exemplary significance of the philosophy of George Grant. Horowitz argued that 'the relative strength of socialism is related to the relative strength of toryism' because of the communitarian ethic of both in distinction from the individualist ethic of liberalism which predominates in the United States.[2] Canadian distinctness lies in the vibrancy of the concept of community in its political culture. Horowitz was aware that his thesis buttressed the Innisian economic explanation for an interventionist state. 'Of course it was [economically] "necessary" to make use of the state in Canada. The question is: why did this necessity not produce ideological strain?'[3] This communitarian component has the consequence that Canadian society is more tolerant, since it accepts greater ideological diversity, and is more inclined to address social issues through state action – which even affects Canadian liberalism.[4] 'In Canada the centre party emerged triumphant over its enemies on the right and the left. Here, then, is another aspect of English Canada's uniqueness: it is the only society in which Liberal Reform faces the challenge of socialism *and* emerges victorious. The English-Canadian fragment *is* bourgeois. The toryism and the socialism are "*touches.*"'[5] The philosophical epitome of this communitarian emphasis in a bourgeois society might well be George Grant's commitment to tradition and the conservation of Canadian particularity, on the one hand, combined with a thoroughgoing moral egalitarianism, on the other.

The definition of Canada as a 'vertical mosaic' was developed by sociologist John Porter in the 1960s at roughly the same time as the Red Tory thesis emerged. The title of his study, *The Vertical Mosaic*, was initially intended as the title of a chapter dealing with the relationship between ethnicity and social class. 'As the study proceeded, however, the hierarchical relationship between Canada's many cultural groups became a recurring theme in class and power.'[6] Porter presented detailed studies of interlocking elites which were imbedded with cultural groups in complex ways. The dominant British elite, for example, was often resented by French Canadians and newer minority groups. Nevertheless, 'the elites of French Canada have worked with the British to create the kind of society that Quebec is.'[7] Canadian studies of social power have tended to focus on this 'recurring theme' of the relationship between ethnicity and social class until the present day.

The term 'mosaic' was immediately appropriated in official documents, and both utilized and criticized in academic discussions, referring to multiculturalism. While there was, of course, no lack of celebratory literature – usually through comparison to the homogenizing idea of the 'melting pot' that predominated in the United States – it was often argued that no genuine mosaic, or multiculturalism, obtained due to class inequality, state regulation, or racial prejudice. While this point was worth making in its own terms, it was often overlooked that these were not opposed terms in Porter's analysis but mutually reinforcing ones in which 'speculatively, it might be said that the idea of an ethnic mosaic, rather than the idea of the melting pot, impedes the processes of social mobility.'[8] The mosaic character of multiculturalism, which distinguishes Canada from the United States, tends to be interpreted as a proposed utopia, in order to be denied that status, when for Porter it was a term directly linked to the 'verticality' of class and elite power.

It has been characteristic of debates about the specific and distinct cultural identity of English Canada to confuse the definition of distinctness with the proposal of an intended, or even achieved, social good. It may well be that we should promote our distinctiveness, though this does not follow automatically, and it may well be suspected that whatever distinctiveness the English-Canadian cultural identity has, it will, like any other cultural identities, contain its specific dangers and evils as well as goods. Porter himself argued in liberal individualist fashion that 'the organization of society on the basis of rights that derive from group membership is sharply opposed to the concept of a society based on citizenship, which has been such an important aspect in the development of modern societies ... Citizenship rights are essentially universalistic whereas group rights are essentially particularistic.'[9] In this key case, which tests the limits of the discourse of cultural identity, distinctiveness was analysed as a defect rather than an advantage. This was possible only through analysing identity in strictly 'sociological' terms, that is to say, as an empirical fact, and abstracting from the procedures of identification which turn such facts into cultural politics.

The theme of communication as defining the specific and distinct cultural identity of English Canada is of more recent origin. Though perhaps implicit in Harold Innis's late works dealing with communication, these works themselves did not address Canada directly. Also, it emerged only peripherally in the work of Marshall McLuhan, who followed up Innis's communication studies. Recently, however, it has become increasingly popular, and persuasive, to see the later focus on communication as continuing Innis's early political-economic studies and as indicating a distinct feature of Canadian history itself. Innis was not just concerned with transportation of goods but with the way in which communication media structured relations of space and time and thus the perception and thought of those within a given media complex. It has been argued that this concern derives from 'a Canadian context that initially generated interest in the transformation and breakdown of empires and the emergence of nation states.'[10] McLuhan generalized this insight into a theory of foreground-background, or explicit-implicit, relations, oriented to the question of how the new can be perceived or understood as new, rather than being dragged back into pre-existing moulds. Phrased in this way, communication is concerned with the construction of dominant manners of perceiving and the conditions under which such dominant manners come into crisis and alter.

For the difficult perception of the new as new, in McLuhan's words, 'borderlines, as such, are a form of political "ecumenism," the meeting place of diverse worlds and conditions. ... Canada is a land of multiple borderlines, of which Canadians have probed very few. These multiple borderlines constitute a low-profile identity, since, like the territory, they have to cover a lot of ground ... The borderline is an area of spiralling repetition and replay, both of inputs and feedback, both of interlace and interface, an area of "double ends joined," of rebirth and metamorphosis.'[11] McLuhan's articulation of the communication theory pushes to the limit, as does Porter's negative evaluation of ethnicity, the discourse of English-Canadian cultural identity itself. 'If a U.S. citizen so chose, Canada could become an enormous psychic theme park; something like a Hollywood set that simultaneously links the past with the present, the city with the wilderness.'[12] For McLuhan, Canadian distinctiveness comes to serve solely as a well of escapism or nostalgia for American tourists, but note that this argument would not work if the language difference of French Canada were taken into account: such a difference would present the American tourist with more difficulties than a theme park.

Even this short survey should serve to indicate several key themes in the four theses concerning the distinctiveness of English Canada: (1) empire, power, dominant modes of perception and thought; (2) transportation, communication, construction of new modes of perception and thought; and (3) community, ethnicity, forms of collective action, especially through the national state. These themes are mutually reinforcing, rather than exclusive, and have served to define a discursive space within which debates about the specific and distinct cultural identity of English Canada have taken place. My interest at this point is in the discursive space and not with the debates themselves.

The discursive space of English-Canadian cultural identity came into existence through a double slippage: between English Canada and Canada and between distinctiveness and the good. A slide, or slippage, is a linguistic term that indicates a conceptual uncertainty and thus a theoretical failure, though it may also indicate a rhetorical success. It consists in slipping from one meaning of a term to another without noting the shift. Indeed, the very facility and invisibility of the slide is a defining feature of the discourse itself which serves to indicate its limits. I occasionally, though somewhat inaccurately, refer to the two slides in question as 'assumptions.' Whereas an assumption usually refers to an unstated underlying premise in a statement, a 'slide' refers to a characteristic of a 'discourse,' which is not a single statement but an organized field of statements. In a certain sense one may characterize a slide as covering an assumption hidden in a discourse, if we understand an assumption in a more existential sense as a blind spot within a certain way of life.

In the case of the discourse of English-Canadian cultural identity, the two slides were as follows. It was often unclear whether the object of analysis was Canada or English Canada, because English Canada was taken to stand for Canada outright. In addition, the argument for distinctiveness was taken as sufficient evidence that there was something here worth preserving.

It is sufficient indication that this discourse has come upon its historical closure that these two assumptions are no longer possible. The self-assertion of Quebec and First Nations in the period since the 1960s has made it obvious that English Canada is only part of the nations-state of Canada. The historical closure was prefigured by the limits of the discourse itself during the period of its dominance. Porter's liberal individualist rejection of ethnicity and communitarianism and McLuhan's interpretation of distinctiveness as entertainment show that the main accounts of English-Canadian uniqueness simply assumed that its 'Canada' was a positive good to be protected and expanded. In an age of globalization, which has inaugurated the taking-apart, or un-building, of the Canada in which this discourse was situated, such an assumption is no longer possible.

The discourse concerning the cultural identity of English Canada in the affirmative mode, in which distinctiveness was taken to be a social good, contains these key elements: a defence of particularity and locality, a critique of empire, a focus on new forms of social communication, and a communitarian conception of the social good. While these elements are combined in different ways and with different emphases by individual thinkers, their combination points to the central and distinctive component of English-Canadian political culture in which modern claims to independence and equality are seen as possible only within a tradition and community that have pre-modern roots.

This is not only a uniquely English-Canadian intellectual tradition; it is also expressive of the founding institutional arrangements that brought Canada into being, the relations whereby Canada was, in an active sense, instituted. The east-west spatial extension of the railway and of trade routes was set up by the policies of an interventionist federal state. The settlement and resource-extraction economy marked a geographical space that was dominated by a central government embodying a colonial, Dominion, and then Commonwealth, temporal continuity with the British Empire. This delicate balance between a rapid geographical expansion that threatened to burst forth from traditional ties was recuperated by a historical continuity directed by the inheritors of the state–private-industry alliance forged by the empire. Similarly, there was a tension between the allegiance of Canadians to their regions, and to the local possibilities that they contained, and their common identity as citizens oriented through the Ottawa axis that defined most political parties and their social goals. Such recuperation and balance were characteristic of Canada until the Free Trade Agreement (1988) and North American Free Trade Agreement (1994) solidified the breakdown of the *dirigiste* east-west axis on which it was based. This has liberated the tendency, which had always been present but had been held in check by the federal axis, for the separate regions of Canada to become integrated into the South-North pull of the contiguous regions in the United States. For this reason, it is not an exaggeration to see the global neo-liberal, or 'free trade,' era as in fundamental opposition to the forces by which Canada was constructed and maintained. It has initiated our un-building, or deconstruction, and thus the necessity to rethink the relation between locality and a certain universality claimed by the nation-state that may be continued in our own time through the construction of a post-colonial thought.

Beyond the Nations-State

The work of Harold Innis and George Grant illustrates the characteristic way in which a critical, localizing thread has woven itself into English-Canadian thought and history. Through this emphasis a communitarian politics has inserted itself into our political culture and enabled us to survive the destructive individualistic and polarizing effects of modern technology, bureaucracy, and capitalism. Its overwhelming rhetorical figure is that of lament, constructed out of an idealized past which has been lost in the present. Its conservative character is based on this look backward which opened up a radical critique of the present world system, which Innis called 'space-dominating' and Grant called 'technological' and whose main political characteristics were an atomistic liberalism combined with American imperialism. This critique implied a communitarian, even pre-modern, ethical standpoint from which to measure the world system, which Innis found in the notion of an oral tradition, based in face-to-face communication, which emphasized historical continuity and local innovation. The main contribution of Grant was the development of a concept of 'particularity' which legitimized non-universal attachments as necessary incarnations of a universal good.

Grant's concept of particularity was introduced to defend Canadian autonomy against the international claims of the American empire. As he said, 'In this era when the homogenizing power of technology is almost unlimited, I do regret the disappearance of indigenous traditions, including my own. It is true that no particularism can adequately incarnate the good. But is it not also true that only through some particular roots, however partial, can human beings first grasp what is good and it is the juice of such roots which for most men sustain their partaking in a more universal good?'[13] While the main intent of this passage was to defend the legitimacy of particularity, and the task of bringing it to thought, it is also clear that it is not good to be enclosed within a particularism. Here we may distinguish between particularism – which by excluding universality elevates particular experiences to the level of a false universality, and is thus an ethnocentrism, parochialism, or even fundamentalism – and particularity, which refers to a recovery of the particular from its forgetting, or loss, in such a way that one may both accept and love one's particularity and also pass beyond it toward a new universality.

Harold Innis also incorporated a localizing turn into his thinking because claims to universality were seen as justifying monopolies of knowledge. He argued that 'the conservative power of monopolies of knowledge compels the development of technological revolutions in the media of communication in marginal areas.'[14] The creativity of marginality was the basis for Innis's re-evaluation of the oral tradition as a hidden source of innovation and stability in Western civilization. In one of his notes he wrote: 'Oral tradition more powerful on frontier and penetrates press and newspaper which cuts under conservative elements.'[15] It seems that claims to universality rooted in the dominance of empire are not only exclusive but also rest upon the hidden and unappreciated resources of particularity and locality.

In taking up the question of the concept of locality, my argument will press toward a clearer articulation of the emergence of universalizations from a particular tradition. This tension – up and down, we might say, or back and forward – not only cannot be avoided but is a necessary aspect of trying to *think* here. Insofar as thought requires categories that supersede their application, the moment of universalization cannot be avoided. Insofar as application is not mere application of pre-existing categories, but rather generates potential categories that would situate the tradition of thought reflexively, there develops a tension between the poles of particularity and universalization such that when one is pushed to a greater extreme, the other is similarly taken toward its limit. In turning to the concept of locality, which has hidden behind arguments about Canada and the world, one is pushed to reframe the world through universalizations deriving from our particularity.

This argument suggests that the recent turn to locality in philosophy, politics, and social criticism is not a simple mood soon to be replaced by a pendulum swing back to globality, nationality, or universality. Rather, it is a characteristic, innovative, and necessary shift of attention that deeply unsettles the assumptions of the social order and that has a privileged place both in the tradition of English-Canadian thought and in that of contemporary social movements. It thus contains the possibility of a discovery of new relations between locality and universalization, between near and distant, in which we may glimpse beyond the limitations of the current social order. Locality is, in this sense, a dis-ordering, a de-construction, which opens a new possibility. But this new possibility can only become clear if we shake clear of the opposition of locality and universality as settled within the current order, and begin from locality in order to discover the universalizing process from which the distant might be recovered without losing locality. I want to ask: What is a concept of locality that does not submit to an abstract and homogenizing universality? What emergent concept of universalization would not abstract from and dominate locality?

There is a contradiction in the tradition of English-Canadian thought insofar as its principled and universalizing defence of locality was hinged exclusively to a politics oriented to the federal state.[16] This claim seems to me obviously true when one looks at the work of Grant and Innis as a whole, and especially at the left-nationalist politics that drew its inspiration from them.[17] It depends mainly on the claim that there is a slippage in their writings, and in their thinking, from the general claim to the instance of the federal state. Put otherwise, they assume that the only relevant particularity is the Canadian state in the international arena, whereas their defence of particularity is principled and universalizing and therefore not limited to this one application.

In *Lament for a Nation*, George Grant asked: 'How can a faith in universalism go with the desire for the continuance of Canada? The belief in Canada's continued existence has always appealed against universalism. It appealed to particularity against the wider loyalty to the continent.'[18] But if an argument for the continued existence of Canada must appeal to the rights of particularity, why cannot the rights of particularity as instantiated in the cities, regions, ethnicities, or other localities, be appealed to against the Canadian state? Why, indeed, is the Canadian state any better an example of particularity than the many and diverse local attachments within it, or the other 'localities' that have been articulated by social movements?

The slippage in the work of Harold Innis is more difficult to locate because he was a social scientist rather than a philosopher, and thus the ethico-political status of his conceptual categories was never broached as an issue. It is an important methodological, epistemological, and ethical question for social science to ask the extent to which its conceptual structure can be independent of ethical and political commitments. However this may be in general, the concepts of oral tradition and empire in Innis are not only analytical but also ethico-political categories that give such significance to the whole context of his arguments. Consider the following quote, where it is hard to imagine what the effect of the argument would be if its categories were interpreted as independent of ethical and political significance: 'The guarantee of freedom of the press under the Bill of Rights in the United States and its encouragement by postal regulations has meant an unrestricted operation of commercial forces and an impact of technology on communication tempered only by commercialism itself ... Canadian publications supported by the advertising of products of American branch plants and forced to compete with American publications imitate them in format, style and content. Canadian writers must adapt themselves to American standards. Our poets and painters are reduced to the status of sandwich men.'[19] Here we can see that the defence of locality and the inventiveness of oral tradition allowed Innis to criticize the suppression of public communication in Canada by American commercialism, even though it is not deployed to criticize commercialism within Canada or elitism within the institutions of the Canadian federal state. While Innis did recognize the particularity of regions within Canada due to the different histories of staple resource extraction, he tended to subsume this under relations between Canada and the United States. 'American branch factories, exploiting nationalism and imperialism in Canada, were in part responsible for agitation in regions exploited by the central area and for regional controversies.'[20] But if the case of Innis regarding this contradiction remains somewhat contestable, due to the innovative role of the periphery in his thought, it is not so in that of Grant, and even less so with regard to the left-nationalism that was the main political inheritance of the social and political thought of English Canada and which regarded the federal state as its central political actor.

With these quotations and comments I have tried to give some substance to my suggestion that English-Canadian social and political thought contains a contradiction: on the one hand, it defends particularity, or localism, in principle and universally; on the other hand, it hinges this defence to a politics oriented exclusively to the national federal state, which is local only in relation to the imperialistic forces of another state. This contradiction implies an acceptance, even if unstated, of the homogenizing forces of the Canadian state itself and consequently often tended toward an idealized portrayal of its history as if it were less marred by internal violence and colonization than other nation-states. The romantically imagined purity of our one place wipes away the conquests from which it was born, and its persisting inequality, through the overweening comparison to greater, and more compromised, international powers. If my claim that this tradition limited itself through substituting the Canadian nation-state for locality in general has any validity, it implies that an immanent critique of this tradition must understand locality in a much wider sense and theorize the new, anticipatory concept of universalization that it contains.

The achievement of a concept of universality was an *accomplishment* in human history that required the separation of the particularities of a single way of life from an assumed and invisible ethnocentrism. Thus, the move to locality must be understood as a *return*, an attempt to *recover* the local, which means that it has been covered up and forgotten. It has been covered up by a formally abstract conception of space and universality that arose with modern science and technology. Within such formal abstraction space is understood as homogeneous and quantitative due to the abstraction from the qualitative differences of places. Thus, we may distinguish space from place. Any place is arbitrary from the point of view of space, and its qualitative components are considered to be simply subjective projections by an internal self without spatial extension. A recovery of the qualitative experience of place is thus part of a criticism of formal abstraction and of the ceding of practical life to scientific-technical imperatives that is characteristic of modernity.

This has affected the concept of criticism itself. For a long time we have sought to break through the limitations of our place and time toward a larger and more inclusive conception. We say, for example, that we must 'get beyond,' or 'move outside,' our preconceptions in order to be able to criticize them, to be able to 'see them from a distance' and not be constrained within them. This moving away from oneself toward the distance is perhaps the oldest rhetorical figure in social criticism, older than the specific form it takes in modernity, which relies on an objectivistic form of reflection for the notion of passing beyond one's own particularity towards more universal and inclusive conceptions. Such passing beyond the particular to the universal is inherent in the very idea of a concept which was discovered in Greek antiquity (and is thus probably a necessary moment of thought). We thus see, for example, that people who act very differently from us, who believe in strange gods or forces, are really very much like ourselves when we utilize the capacity to see our own practices, beliefs, and gods as particular and local, and therefore as not the only valid form that practices, beliefs, and gods can take. Such universality was enlightening precisely because it loosened the connection between the particularities of one's own experience and the conception of human experience outright. One's own became an example, another case study, at the moment that the previously strange other became an example too. The universal, which was previously compacted with one's own in an ethnocentrism that could not be aware of itself as such, retreated one step in abstraction so that both one's own and the other could be seen to be equally valid examples of the universal.

In our own time this figure of criticism, and this movement from particular to universal, has come upon a limitation. It is unlikely to be exhausted entirely, since it will always be necessary to discover that one's own ways are not the only human, or reasonable, ways and therefore that others have a right to their ways, and that such ways are equally as human as ours. But there are reasons now to suspect that this figure of criticism, and this conception of universality, is not adequate to the tasks that press upon us now, and thus that the concept of enlightenment it legitimates needs to be rethought through the experience of recovering place from objectified space and so to open the possibility of belonging in one's place, rather than merely occupying a certain space.

It is crucially important now to oppose the pervasive tendencies to cynicism and hectic consumption through the recovery, preservation, and appropriation of ethical norms themselves. Such norms are embedded in the religious, philosophical, and political traditions that are being liquidated today by the corporatization of artistic, cultural, and intellectual life – not least, though not solely, in the universities. In this, it is not so much a matter of preserving specific norms themselves but of preserving the cultural heritage whereby norms have been, and are, formed. If locality is an important element of contemporary critique, then there is a continued importance of the preservation and critical appropriation of cultural heritages. In this sense, the cultural and political heritages of nations imbricated in the historical construction of Canada are important resources for the construction and maintenance of ethical norms whose violation is now at issue. One must recover English-Canadian social and political thought, show its limitations, and argue for its extension all at once. This can be achieved through the intellectual operation known as immanent criticism through which this book has been constructed. The historical recovery and critical focus of immanent criticism are rooted in a contemporary project: only by inhabiting the 'here' that has made us can we develop a critique adequate to the new tasks that now confront us. The ground of a philosophical defence of such inhabitation is in a phenomenology of locality, but we have to go into the conceptual basis of terms like place, locality, and so forth in more detail to get beyond the form in which these were settled in the period dominated by the discourse of the distinctiveness of English Canada.[21]

A Phenomenology of Locality

Our dictionaries tend to define locality as a place or site, which no doubt flirts with separatism and purism. I want, rather, not to think place as such, but to think location. If a place were truly separate, or isolate, it could not be located. The term 'location' as a verb is better here, meaning 'locating' or 'being located' (OED), which connotes an activity of locating and thus contains at least an implicit relation to other places. Location requires a placing *in relation to* other places. Thus, it is not only a matter of connection, but *the connection as it emerges from and defines a specific place*. While location retains the reference to a single place, it refers to situating this place in its relation to other places, especially those other places that have significance for this one.

Thinking location in this sense attempts what might be called 'locative thinking.' The locative case denotes the place where an action occurs. Thinking in the locative case is a thinking which is permeated by the awareness of its own place, that will not abandon itself to abstract space, but neither can be restrained within a given place and defines itself in its relation to other places of significance. Locative thinking is a thinking that does not simply occur somewhere, but whose location is integral to the meaning of what is thought. Locative thinking dwells in the moment in which connection is made to other places beginning from here. It thinks through English-Canadian problems as a practice that forges non-administrative relations to other places. These relations define our location in a larger world. Particularity, as distinguished from particularism, thus corresponds to the emphasis on location over place, and locative thinking, which can be described as *the thinking of the particular as it leads outward to other particulars*, would avoid the dangers of a self-enclosed concentration on place (as it might be expressed in separatism or Fundamentalism) and contain the possibility of a universalization.

I want now to fix more clearly on how locality is experienced as locality – what is the essence of locality, such that it begins from a qualitatively experienced place but leads on and connects with other places of significance. Location is place caught in the act of leading elsewhere. In order for locality to lead on to another place, it must involve an experience of place that is not enclosed but opens out and also an experience of another place to which it opens out. The phenomenon of 'leading-outward' requires an 'opening-out' and a 'there' to which the opening opens. Such a leading-outward means that one can also come back, that there is an experience of 'coming-back,' or 'returning-toward' the 'home place,' that defines particularity as such. Notice that, both in leading-outward and in coming-back, there is a double aspect to the movement. As movement, it is in a certain place but headed somewhere else. This is traversal. Movement has a goal – in one case, the other place where one is headed and, in the other, the home place to which one is returning. The goal, be it there or home, can be understood as a place since it is a destination and thus the end of movement. In thus associating place with stasis, the phenomenon of locality emerges more clearly. Place begins where movement ceases and is transformed into locality where movement begins. The essence of locality is in the opening-out and returning-toward. It is the movement between places that allows them to be situated in relation to each other. Locality overcomes separation and thus avoids the problem of Indifference or Fundamentalism. Locality is the constituting of movement prior to the definition of places.

Location requires these two, an opening-out and returning-toward, because movement contains the possibility of return even though the two are never symmetrical. A rapids that can be shot one way requires a portage on return. In our time, much intellectual and practical energy has gone into showing the possibility and actuality of return due to the dominance of abstract space over the imagination of modernity. Thus, we are rediscovering locality as a phenomenon of return toward place. Inhabitation of one's home place is the goal. The necessity of return stems from something having gone wrong with the journey – its immersion in the objectification of the world which has cut off its relation to its origin – such that we need to turn back toward our original place. This is an essential movement of the world of our time. However, with one's sight fixed upon returning home, it is easy to pass over another, equally important, aspect of our situation. While our goal is home, we are still in movement. It is the movement that will bring us home, and the movement of return is what will situate home in relation to other places and will free us from the original illusion that our home is the only significant place. Originally, this illusion was merely naive and not dangerous, an ethnocentrism that had not yet encountered others. Now, it becomes Fundamentalism – the conviction that encountered others are congenitally and inevitably wrong or evil. Consequently, it also motivates others to avoid the return and remain Indifferent and homeless. In fixing on locality, on the movement that defines place, we can walk with the crucial tendency of our time toward the recovery of home without falling into either side of this illusion.

Location requires a placing *in relation to* other places. Perhaps we can derive some direction from ordinary English usage at this point. If I say, 'meet me at the café,' which is a place, my interlocutor might respond '*which* café?' To say, '*the* café' would suffice if we were in the café, or if there were only one café, or if we always met at the same café, or, in short, if the word 'café' named a unique and therefore unmistakable place. But, if I want to locate this place – that is to say, put it into relation with other places – I might add 'the café across from the train station.' This would probably suffice if there were only one train station, or if there were only one train station close that pertains to our neighbourhood. Otherwise, I might say 'across from the train station *downtown*,' or 'on the Drive, of course.' In each case, a specification is introduced, if necessary, in order to locate the place in relation to other places. If the place is referred to within a locality shared by speaker and interlocutor, then it needs no further specification. If further specification is required, it is because the locality is not equally shared, or assumed, by both. In such a case, the place is located, or defined in relation to a plurality of places.

Thus, it is not only a matter of connection but the connection as it [illegible] a specific place. While location retains the reference to a single place, it refers to situating this place in its relation to other places, especially those other places that have significance for this one. To specify the café by saying 'across from the station' means that the station becomes a place from which the café as a place is situated. But here the station is not meant as a place in the same sense that the café is meant as a place. The station is not so much a place as a reference to a location. The location is not the station as such, but the interplay of places in and around the station, its vicinity. The station here stands as a name for the entire location. In another example, of course – say in referring to the station *downtown* – the station might be a place defined through another location. This example brings out the key characteristic of a location. It cannot be defined except in relation to a place. While location is a certain connection between a plurality of places, it cannot be seen either as an aggregate of places or as something standing over against place as such. We might say that location is a place caught in the act of leading elsewhere. It is a place that takes on the role of specifying a relation between places. It is a place that comes to constitute the locality that gathers places together. Thus, it is not only a matter of connection, but *the connection as it emerges from a specific place*. While location retains the reference to a single place, it refers to situating this place in its relation to other places, especially those other places that have significance for this one.

This connection, whereby a place stands for the interplay between places that constitutes a location, shows the special character of the nearness of a neighbourhood. That which is face to face in the now is that which is near in the sense of belonging-together in the same locality. The café is near to the station because the station is a locality where one can walk easily from one side of the road to another and where one can get easily by car or bus. A café might be 'objectively' in space and time nearer to the station but not be in the same locality if it were on the other side of a highway that could not be crossed on foot, for example. The locality is constituted by a nearness that means the co-accessibility of places. Similarly, a place – such as a glass-panel factory – might be close in objective space and time to the station but not be part of the locality because we pass the station coming and going on our daily business and would not genuinely encounter a glass-panel factory in that context. Though, of course, a shoe repair shop might well be part of the locality because it is very convenient to pass on the way to work and then to stop at the café to chat with friends. It is the belonging-together that gathers places in the constitution of locality.

I want to now fix more clearly on how locality is experienced as locality, what is the essence of locality, such that it retains a reference to a qualitatively experienced place but leads on and connects with other places of significance. In order for locality to lead on to another place, it must involve an experience of place that is not enclosed but opens out and also an experience of another place to which it opens out. The phenomenon of 'leading-outward' requires an 'opening-out' and a 'there' to which the opening opens. Such a leading-outward means that one can also come back, that there is an experience of 'coming-back,' or 'returning-toward' the 'home place,' or the place from which the neighbourhood takes its reference. Notice that, in leading-outward and in coming-back, there is a double aspect to the movement, but these aspects are not symmetrical. Let us take each movement in turn. The essence of locality is in the opening-out and returning-toward.

Leading-out addresses itself toward a place, whereas the 'place' from which one is led out is not a place but a location – that is to say, a place that is standing for the neighbourhood, or vicinity – insofar as it is not the end, or goal, of situating but that which situates, locates, which orients the outward movement itself. The goal, a 'there,' can be understood as a place since it is a destination and thus the end of movement. Place begins where movement ceases. I am heading toward the café. The movement outward moves smoothly through its location toward a point at which the movement ceases. Locality is the constituting movement prior to the definition of place, not necessarily as origin, but as orientation. In moving-outward, this orientation functions but is not thematic. It is the goal on which attention is focused.

The movement of leading-outward is paired with an asymmetrical movement of returning-toward since it is in the relation between these two that the essence of locality resides. This phenomenology of location accounts for the initial movement of criticism as a movement away from home to other places and for the insufficiency of this model of criticism in our own time. There must be a reversal, a coming-back, which is paired with the movement outward but is not symmetrical to it because home and there appear differently in the two movements.

While leading-outward is smooth, in the sense that it encounters no interruptions in its movement toward there, returning-toward experiences a border, or a line that is permeable, that interrupts the smoothness of movement. In the moment of return, the line is constituted as location congeals into a place. The 'there' was defined in outward movement, while home remained unthematic. In the movement of return, the 'there' has been defined and thus functions both as place and orientation – thematic orientation – while home is the goal of the return. As the location of home becomes place, the return is constituted as a movement between places, from there to here, which are divided by a line that separates them as distinct places. Returning home is a way that crosses this line. The station that defines a neighbourhood – which is thus not taken as a station in the sense of a single place, but as defining a vicinity, a location – becomes through this movement of return a place, a station. The here is defined as here in the movement of return from there. It is the line that creates the border between here and there. This line is created by the shrinking from location to place in which the inter-ness of the interplay disappears. The movement of return is a kind of shrinking in which the original orientation that defines a vicinity becomes a place such that distance between here and there appears. Thus, the 'original' here, which is first defined as a place in the movement of return when it becomes a goal, is first defined as a 'there' –

ative of inhabitation. I will try to explain the history of the colonial and post-colonial demand for writing in Canada in order to show why locative universalization is demanded from contemporary philosophy.

We may begin by recalling Northrop Frye's famous generalization that Canadian literature is, or at least was, a continuous meditation on 'Where is here?'[22] Frye's observation is not surprising since any colonial literature must begin by facing the task of finding its place while at the same time using tools which derive from elsewhere. In the first place, this is likely to be, in terms taken from Harold Innis's dependency theory, a centre–periphery relation. That is to say, the attempt to write here places itself in relation to a there in which the categories of explanation and description – the myths, Frye would say – have been defined through an ongoing tradition. It is thus a culture of dependency even though its contents meditate on here. The first attempt places a new colonial content within the categories of empire and is fixed on a meditation on where it takes place. It is interested in writing itself, but it cannot yet imagine that its experience can generate categories as well as content.

As the imperial tie slackens, and a post-colonial literature emerges, whose main task will be to generate from this place the categories from which this place can be understood, that is, to develop its own tradition. It will thus take a step back from the question 'Where is here?' in order to ask through what categories of thought and experience the question can be properly formulated. Thus, the question becomes 'What are the myths through which we can understand here?' or 'What is the map that defines where is here?' Clear as he was about the structuring influence of myth, Frye might have asked this question, but he did not, since he remained convinced of the straightforward universality of the biblical myth. At this point one is beyond a culture of dependency, and thus capable of criticizing it, but no viable alternative yet presents itself. The philosophy of George Grant and the political economy and communication theory of Harold Innis were at this stage and thus immensely critical, though ultimately unsatisfying. The critique of received imperial categories has begun, the search for new and independent categories is underway, and thus an intense and creative work is possible. But, in the absence of discovering even a single fixed point in mythical or categorial space, this creative energy falls back into the imperial categories that it attempts to overcome. Authors writing from out of the experience of this tension can thus be interpreted in two ways, each of which has its truth – in terms of the creative moment which impels them forward or through the imperial categories to which they finally return. Thus, while Grant wrote profoundly and intensely of the experience of wilderness that separates ex-European Canadians from their ancestors, wilderness as such never became a category of thought through which he interpreted the history or task of philosophy. Frye wrote from within the same tension. While his investigation of Canadian literature was both wide and deep, he never found in it anything to add to European mythology. Innis surveyed with an eagle's eye the biases that structured Canadian political economy and the history of empires, but he never proposed an understanding of either economy or communication that might substantiate the possibility of local independence – orality was a *critical* category, and that only; he was not an anarchist. Perhaps one could generalize so far as to suggest that our greatest thinkers and interpreters of Canadian culture thus far have been great insofar as they have inhabited this tension but have not been able to fix a single point in post-colonial categorial space.

The question for contemporary thought should now be clear: Is there any post-colonial writing in Canada, a writing that encompasses the task of writing about everywhere from here – that is to say, of proposing myths, or categories of explanation and description, that illuminate the human condition as such? At this intense point, one is asking 'Where are the maps from here applicable?' or 'To what extent can our maps illuminate the world?'

Since English-Canadian philosophy is a form of literature, even if philosophy is not exhausted by its literary expression, it will tend to pass through the same three-step development – bearing in mind, of course, that the three will often overlap and be present in the same work. There is, though, a prior ground zero which still persists among those who refuse to face the impetus behind this development. Such would be a philosophy that is merely *in* Canada, that takes place here only in mathematical terms of spatial and temporal extension. It is here only because it is nowhere else and takes on both its problems and the terms for posing them from a pre-existing tradition. Once the pressure of thinking and writing here begins to assert itself, it will at first tend to be simply philosophy *about* Canada and the issues it poses. Terms and categories will still be inherited from another tradition. Next, the terms and categories will themselves need to be rooted in the historical experience from which the problems develop. This involves a philosophy *of* Canada, a philosophy whose terms are universalizations derived from its particularity and which strain to produce and articulate a tradition.

Finally, the intensity of this effort can produce the demand that this tradition add to the terms and categories of understanding which illuminate the human condition as such. To do this, the tradition must ask 'What is philosophy?' since the nature of the enterprise itself can no longer be simply taken over.

Colonial and post-colonial philosophy thus struggles with the relationship of particularity and universalization, in which it begins by straining to become more than an application of an existing tradition and ends, in the many senses of that word, by discovering the universalizations which propose the form of binding-together that defines the tradition. A tradition is not a sealed vessel. It is formed both through influences deriving from outside and incorporated within as well as through influences from within that become interesting developments elsewhere. A tradition is always permeated by influences stemming from other traditions. The unity of a tradition, as compared with other traditions, is not so much in their content (though emphases do often differ in different traditions, some seem to immediately ask epistemological questions, others to dwell on political implications) but in the *form of binding-together*, that is to say, the categories of explanation and description, through which the internal relationship between elements is constructed. The form of binding-together that makes a tradition in English Canada is, I have argued, the concern with particularity, community, and locality within the context of an emergent universalization.

At its apogee, a philosophical tradition will need to define in its own terms 'What is a philosophical tradition?' A major danger in such an effort at an independent philosophical tradition will be the tendency to innovation for its own sake. Moreover, this is not a danger that can be simply averted, since conservatism in this case would not be tradition-sustaining but tradition-undermining. When one's tradition is in the future, brakes can only be found there also. The danger of reckless innovation can only be checked by pushing on to the final question. This history of the demand placed on writing by the transition from a colonial to a post-colonial condition leads us to recall that we began thinking about Canada with terms and categories inherited from the empire and suggests that, at least as a first step, we must recall how they came here. Thus, in our own time, we must begin not with here but with the movement toward here, movement here, and movement leading-outward toward other places.

Those interested in taking this thinking forward must look back especially at the moments when this imperial legacy encountered

Others, when its movement paused. And the look backward requires also that one look ahead, leading-outward toward the world, with the terms and categories upon which our experience insists. The role of the critical intellectual is not to be right, nor to propose policy, but to redeem the metaphors thrust on us by our history, and risk movement. Such an acceptance of the struggles inherent in one's belonging, a turning of them toward universality, is what turns fate into destiny. The destiny of English Canada is in the role that a defence of particularity and locality can offer to the world, but such a defence can no longer be satisfied with the claim of its distinctiveness in defining English Canada. It must risk a universalizing defence of locality as such.

3 Critique of Empire

English-Canadian culture has come upon a moment of decision. It can no longer assume that it stands for Canada as a whole. Canada must be understood not as a nation-state (in the singular) but as a nations-state in which, at the very least, Quebec and First Nations also have constitutive roles. It is this moment that requires us to focus on English Canada itself as a form of identity and thus pose clearly and radically the question of its relation to the other constituent parts. Moreover, one can also no longer assume that the historically constituted, distinctive identity of English Canada contains a sufficient argument for its continued existence. One must address its identity in the context of what is good for humans without restriction – that is to say, pose the philosophical question 'What is the good life?' While a contemporary exploration of justice may still take its negative, critical bearings from the critique of empire upon which that identity was predicated, the contemporary relevance of the critique of empire must be demonstrated rather than assumed. If one focuses on what is specific and distinctive in the critique of empire characteristic of English-Canadian social and political thought, one encounters a suspicion of history articulated through an archaic encounter with wilderness, a defence of locality articulated as a critique of imperial space, and a defence of particularity as that which is overlooked and sacrificed in the universal claims of the centre.

In this chapter I want to sharpen the significance of these characteristics by showing that they have entered into the constitution of Canadian culture only in an officially domesticated form. The import of this critical point is to argue that a more adequate account based on subsistence and sustainability maintains a historical solidarity with the assertion of the significance of place and independence to identity that we associate with the Rebellions led by Louis Riel. This argument suggests, in a manner which will be taken up in the next chapter, that the very difference between a sovereign identity and a minority depends upon the history of conflict through which the assumptions of empire have succeeded, been denied, or, more often, been limited and compromised by the defenders of inhabitation.

The Constitutive Paradox of Cultural Identity

When one reflects upon the cultural identity of English Canada in a contemporary context, one immediately confronts a paradox that derives from the inseparability of cultural identities *in* English Canada and the identity *of* English Canada itself. Sub-national identities and social movement identities cannot be placed *within* English Canada in any sense analogous to the sense in which they can be placed within 'Canada.' Since English Canada is not an organized polity, but a fragment, it cannot function as a container in the way that nation-states are normally assumed to function as a container for that which occurs 'inside' their borders. The fact that the identity of English Canada is very rarely posed as a question is itself the main issue. Or, put in terms of my previous analysis of the discourse of English-Canadian identity, the real contemporary issue has been hidden by the slippage in meaning between Canada and English Canada. Moreover, when it is posed as an issue, quite often the supposedly 'sub-national' identities come to stand for it: English Canada is often defined by its diversity, multiculturalism, and so forth that are claimed to occur 'within' it.

This might help to explain the observation that the current situation consists in a proliferation of identities whose relations are unfixed and therefore combine in new forms. Heated political and intellectual debates concerning cultural identity have become a sign of our times. Identities are unfixed because there is no hegemonic force – no longer 'Canada' not (yet?) 'English Canada' – capable of linking them under a single umbrella. Identities proliferate and enter into new relations in a moment of crisis when they are not fixed by a hegemonic force.

'English Canada' is neither a nation-state nor a regional grouping with representative political institutions. Its cultural identity tends to disappear as an object of analysis. Questions of the identity of English Canada have tended to aim either 'above' at 'Canada' or 'below' toward a sub-national identity such as region, province, city, and so forth, or 'outside' toward a non-national identity such as feminism or other gender-based identities, environmentalism, or other social movement–based identities, and so forth. English Canada has only a minor degree of consciousness of itself which has arisen recently in relation to the self-assertive politics of Quebec and First Nations. Even the name *English* Canada is problematic: the rest of Canada, Canada without Quebec, and other circumlocutions, register this difficulty. Given that the name does not refer to the origins of its citizens considered individually, but to the language of everyday interaction and the institutional consequences of this dominance, the name seems appropriate. It also has the advantage of pointing to the fact that the origin of this dominance is not, as some apologists would have it, in ordinary convenience, but in the legacy of the British Empire. Thus, if one can speak of the cultural identity of English Canada, one must keep in mind that it is an identity that has expressed itself mainly through an identification with *Canada* as such – thus often rendering invisible the question of its relations to Quebec and First Nations. The slide between English Canada and Canada covers a conceptual confusion that was a historically effective structuring factor in English-Canadian identity. English Canadians took themselves to be simply Canadians outright, thereby hiding the fact that it is the only cultural identity that has not been included into Canada by conquest or treaty. That is to say, the slide operates to obscure the legacy of empire within the Canadian nations-state.

But the problem has an even deeper dimension. To the extent that the cultural identity of English Canada is unaware of itself, lacking self-interpretation, and thus lacking the form of existence of a cultural identity, it is problematic to what extent we can consider other cultural identities as existing *within* English Canada. If an overarching hegemonic identity were fixed, then the hegemonized elements could well be regarded as within it, but to the extent that the (apparently) 'higher' identity is tenuous and unsettled, the so-called 'elements' might be better regarded as 'higher' and the identity 'English Canada' itself might be considered a fragment. It is unclear which identity is the container, or context, and which the content, or hegemonized. This general situation generates a reciprocal definition of identity that I call 'constitutive paradox.' Constitutive paradox occurs whenever there is an absence of hierarchical relation between two identities, but yet they are not simply different, so that they become mutually definitional and, alternatively, each can become content for the other as context, or container.

Prior to the hegemonic crisis which has instituted a constitutive paradox for cultural identity in/of English Canada, the slide between

Canada and English Canada kept national, sub-national, and a-national identities under the hegemonic fixture of the nation-state. Such fixture allows cultural identities to appear natural and therefore unproblematic.

Let me clarify this situation through an account of the 'mode of existence' of cultural identities such that their fixture often predominates through largely stable historical periods but comes into crisis as they end. One may define a personal identity, or a 'self,' as a situated, embodied reflexivity.[1] That is to say, a self is localized in a place distinguished from all that is not-self, and is conscious of itself as so distinct. In order to investigate 'cultural identities' one must respect the specific activities through which such identities are constituted as such without reducing them to identities of another, 'lower,' level such as personal identities. Cultural identities are thus unities, or totalities, whose specific character is destroyed if they are dissolved into their purported components (human individuals) or, for that matter, unified into a 'higher-level' composite. A situated reflexivity gathers its various components neither randomly nor as a mere aggregate but rather through an emphasis – or, conversely, disavowal – of some components over others. Thus some components of the identity are regarded as crucial, others as more peripheral, others as regrettable, and so on. Such modes of self-interpretation may be called *salience*. It is through salience that some components of an identity become badges, or signs, of the identity itself. These signs register the difference of a given identity within the current field of identities. Reflexivity always has this double-sidedness: the inter-relationship of self-interpretation and interpretation of others situates an actor in the social world. The indefinite plurality of the interaction of social identities requires that it be conceptualized as a 'politics of identity' rather than in Hegelian terms as a 'politics of recognition' such as is proposed by Charles Taylor, which leads to conceptualizing the field of identities as a straightforward duality of 'denial and counter-denial.'[2] A Hegelian phrasing assumes the duality of the 'dialectic of self-consciousness' and is thus insufficient to grasp the indefinite plurality of the contemporary field and will likely slide toward the consideration of only 'official' identities.

Self-interpretation of a situated self, whether personal or 'higher-order,' involves action as a necessary and constituent element. The investigation of cultural identities is not primarily about the 'beliefs' that individuals claim to hold when asked but about the activities that the cultural identity undertakes that constitute it as such and which are the basis for self-interpretation. For example, an ethnic cultural identity involves participation in key activities such as festivals, religious (or originally religious) holidays, sacrifices, and so on without which the cultural identity does not exist. Reflection upon these activities by poets, teachers, artists, and cultural workers of all kinds is the self-interpretation that binds the cultural identity into a unity. The media of communication in which these activities and reflections are embodied constitutes the materiality of the self-expression of a cultural identity. Cultural identity depends upon a degree of reflexive 'consciousness of itself,' understood in this concrete manner, which can be either strengthened or weakened depending on its relationships with other cultural identities that overlap or compete. In this sense, cultural identity occurs within an ongoing, socially constitutive, agonistic, rhetorical field.

Cultural identities are articulated by cultural workers in expressions that intervene in the current configuration of the social world and project it forward into a new situation initiating a complex cultural politics of representation: first, *which* identities are represented (and which are marginalized or absent); second, *where* they are represented – whether on a powerful social medium like television or in a coffee shop or around a kitchen table; third, *how* they are represented – which cognitive, perceptual, and social characteristics the medium emphasizes and which it fails to capture; fourth, which characteristics of the cultural identity have been selected as salient and in what way have they been characterized, which also includes the question of *who* represents whom; and fifth, perhaps summing up all the rest, *why* the representation in question has the social impact that it has. While such expressions are often called representations, it would be a misunderstanding to regard them as simply referring to pre-existing identities. For this reason, 'articulation' is often thought to be a more adequate concept. Activities that express, form, and promote cultural identities clearly pertain to the constitution of these identities as such both internally and in their impact on the social world. Thus, a key question for cultural politics is understanding the field of cultural identities in its plurality and historical dynamism. Any investigation of a given identity needs to consider the relationship between a given cultural identity as it has been formed within a prior configuration, its self-constitution through expressions, the change of its identity through such expressions, and, further, its impact upon the subsequent field of cultural identities.

Considering an identity within the field of differences that defines the reciprocal relations of identities implies that an identity is not merely internal – what is nowadays called an 'essentialist' conception – but is formed as what it is in these reciprocal relations. Within any historical period, the reciprocal relations of identities are relatively stable. Or, to put it in terms of theoretical priority: a historical period is constituted by the relative stability of the reciprocal relations between identities. Such a *fixing* of relations of difference can be traced to the institutional arrangements which provide stability among relations of identity beyond the time span of individuals. Analytically, therefore, institutional shifts are the key to historical periodization even though they are often prefigured by social movements which press the identity formations to their limits. Periods of historical crisis and change are characterized by the *unfixing* of relations of identity such that they are cut loose, or float, until a new fixing arrives. Within such a crisis identities proliferate and enter into new relations. English Canada is currently undergoing such a crisis in which there is a proliferation of unfixed identities. If this event of deconstruction, un-building, can be located historically, it should suggest what current configurations herald for a future politics of identity.[3] The discourse of cultural identity of English Canada can be defined on the background of its historical fixture with an aim to defining its contemporary crisis that produces a proliferation of identities without a definitive hierarchical relation.

Therefore every cultural identity normally refers to itself and to the hegemonic force of identity that reigns. A hegemonic identity defines a universal that fixes the place of particular identities. Thus is defined the relation between container and contained, context and content, universal and particular. Ethno-cultural identities are minority identities 'within' English Canada, one may say in this spirit. In times of crisis, in which there is an unfixing, or un-building, this unproblematic relation between particular and universal becomes unsettled. Thus, identities proliferate and enter into new relationships without becoming fixed. The relation between container and contained, context and content, universal and particular is no longer determined.

The cultural identity of English Canada has always been problematic, either in the form in which it was passed over in the slide toward Canada or in the contemporary form in which it is ceded no significant place in the neo-liberal global hegemony. If, despite this evanescence, we pose the question of the relation between English Canada and sub-national identities and social movement identities, then English Canada cannot be assumed as a hegemonic formation and thereby conceived as a container, or context, for these other identities. What English Canada is, or will be, depends in large part on how its relations with these identities might be settled (as well as with the 'external' ones of Quebec and First Nations). The identity of English Canada itself must be held as problematic, questionable, in the same moment that the question of the other identities is raised.

In place of a container–contained, context–content, relation we must therefore conceptualize them as mutually referring: Either might be the container for the other depending on the aspect of the question that is thematized. For example, a more equitable distribution of wealth and power between ethno-cultural groups, or a recognition of the important role of social movement identities in the public realm, might legitimize an overarching English-Canadian identity. In coming to define the content of English-Canadian identity, these others become its container, or context. If an English-Canadian identity could emerge to negotiate a viable space with Quebec and First Nations, and against neo-liberal globalization, then it could serve to protect and develop ethno-cultural and social movement identities. It would become the container for these other contents. In a moment of crisis, the relation goes both ways. It becomes paradoxical.

To give a formal definition: Lacking hegemonic fixture, an identity oscillates paradoxically between being simply a particular identity and being a candidate for content of the universal, hegemonic identity. Its condition of emergence is that an identity is constitutively paradoxical when it cannot be definitively located within a hegemonic fixture of the field of identities. 'Lower' and 'higher' identities can switch places. A particular identity and its purportedly universal hegemonic formation can only be defined reciprocally, and the definition cannot establish in a prior manner which must be assumed in order to provide the definition for the other. Thus, the difficulty is one of how to arrive at the starting point for analysis rather than how to proceed from an established foundation.

This analysis suggests that English-Canadian identity is constitutively paradoxical insofar as its existence depends upon the identities that purportedly comprise it, not as providing the content for a pre-existing container, but for the very existence of the identity of English Canada itself. This means that the identity of English Canada only comes into existence through a political project that would wrest it free of both its submergence into Canada and its dissolution into an international English-language culture dominated by the United States. While the language of fate lends itself to the form of a lament, the language of a political project is self-creation and political will. Its danger is not the defeatism of historical necessity, but a false optimism of the will that would make all projects seem viable. Avoiding this danger requires that the political project be rooted in the historical formation of a people such that through self-creation it confronts its origin in what it has been made. Fate is thus fashioned into destiny, which releases a joy of self-knowing in self-making, but, having cut loose from necessity, remains without guarantee. In such a way English Canada might assume its identity by going forward to meet its transformation to confront new circumstances. This project depends upon a revealing of the past that has its peculiar difficulty in the failure of English Canada to achieve hegemonic fixity. One suspects that the constitutive paradox that this failure bequeaths to questions of identity in/of English Canada reveals a dimension of identity that emerges whenever hegemonies are unsettled. In other words, the un-building of Canada has revealed the constitutive paradox that haunts all cultural identities throughout even their periods of apparent fixity. From the contemporary perspective of this un-building one is motivated to look into the historical process by which it was built and can glimpse the possibilities that were written out by the subordination of particular identities to empire.

In Defence of Louis Riel

It is Louis Riel and the two North-West Rebellions that perhaps most clearly raise the question of the radical outside of empire to which the critical thinker must attend. *The Declaration of the People of Rupert's Land and the North-West* (8 December 1869) begins by affirming the original compact of government:

> Whereas, it is admitted by all men, as a fundamental principle, that the public authority commands the obedience and respect of its subjects. It is also admitted, that a people, when it has no *Government*, is free to adopt one form of Government in preference to another, to give or to refuse allegiance to that which is proposed.[4]

It may be doubted whether the redcoats, the explorers who landed on a shore and claimed all the land touching the sea for their sovereign, or the kings who rule in such a fashion, would make such an admission, but the rest of us might find this a reasonable starting point, especially since there is no recourse to a supposed Enlightenment first condition of God or nature (such as prevailed in the United States). The people of Rupert's Land and the North-West were thrust into this primary condition of choosing their government by a historical event. 'A company of adventurers known as the "Hudson Bay Company," and invested with certain powers, granted by His Majesty (Charles II), established itself in Rupert's Land, and in the North-West Territory, for trading purposes only.' But since there was no other government recognized by the crown, that company took on such a role and, although it 'was far from answering to the wants of the people ... this people ... gave to it a faithful allegiance.' However, without consulting the people, 'contrary to the law of nations, in March, 1869, that said Government surrendered and transferred to Canada all the rights which it had, or pretended to have.' Thus, 'the people of Rupert's Land and the North-West became free and exempt from all allegiance to the said Government' and also 'refuse to recognize the authority of Canada.'

The people claimed the right to choose their government and to exercise the right of self-rule because, first, they had been abandoned; second, they had not been consulted in the transfer of authority; and third, they 'refuse[d] to recognize the authority of Canada, which pretends to have a right to coerce us, and impose upon us a despotic form of government still more contrary to our rights and interests as British subjects.' This mixture of historical and original components is enough to confound the advocates of both ancient and modern constitutions! They are in an original condition because they have been thrust there by a historical event. They assert the right to be consulted in a transfer of sovereignty. This claim cannot be understood to extend to the right to be consulted during normal government. After all, they had accepted the inadequate government of the Hudson's Bay Company. It is the transfer that confers this right, they say. It originates, then, in their being historically thrust into the original condition of selecting a government. They refuse the Canadian government the right to rule them, but what is their reason? It claims to have a right to coerce them and it is of a despotic nature. Do these characterizations provide additional fundamental reasons for their right to choose their own government? Not really. Rather, they *explain* the previous part of the sentence, the refusal to recognize Canada's authority. These, then, are the two reasons for their decision, but the right to make the decision itself is not conferred by their reasons for so deciding. The *Declaration* goes on to point out that they have successfully defended their land from Canada and from neighbouring Indians, but this fact does not confer the legitimacy of their self-rule either. It only establishes the right as a fact. The right to make their own decision stems from the original condition brought forth by their abandonment: transfer without consultation.

The *Declaration* does not explain why the historical condition of abandonment without consultation confers the right to self-rule through the choice of one's government. However, another document by the Provisional Government from the following year does do so. Referring first to their abandonment, to their condition as British subjects, and to the successes of their army, they then state that 'we possess to-day, without partition, almost the half of a continent. The expulsion or annihilation of the invaders has rendered our land natal to its children.'[5] It is their ability to occupy the land, which is proven by the fact that it has become natal to their children, which justifies their right to self-rule. The historical condition of abandonment without consultation confers the right to self-rule through the choice of one's government because the people have inhabited the land. This inhabitation is proven by the fact that their children have no other homeland, that this has become their place. I have dwelt at some length with this remarkable and little-known *Declaration* of self-rule not only because its mixture of British traditional rights and American Enlightenment rights is unprecedented, nor simply because this may go beyond being a mixture to exemplify the historical circumstances under which the original question of government is posed by a people, but because it shows the claim of the periphery to become innovative and independent, to undermine the claim of the empire to provide the rules for negotiation. Their self-foundation reveals the partiality of the empire's rules; it manifests the proposed universality of their self-given rules. It embodies the dream of independence that the New World proposed at the limit of Europe's empires. It punctuates the common but superficial claim that Canada is the most European New World nations-state and reveals the critical polarity between modern and archaic that defines Canadian culture: the most archaic, that inhabitation of the land confers the right to self-rule.

The claim that Canada's history has been oriented around 'community and diversity' originating in the encounter of English and French and continuing through various regional, racial-cultural, and gender struggles up to the present politics of identity does, as far as it goes, sketch the main features of official culture. But it misses the motive for the movement, or 'progress,' of official culture because it ignores the process by which certain available alternatives (which I personify with the name of Riel) were repressed and kept 'outside' and therefore cannot explain the motive which drives official culture but can only accept it as a simple given. It understands civility only as civil peace and order and fails to understand the inherent tendency to complacency, banality, and silence that the continuous history of rights-bearing Englishmen saddles us with. That in Canadian culture which breaks with this complacency is indebted to those who, like Riel, claimed independence 'outside' and provided the motive 'inside' for critique. Thus, the civil version of continuity with empire and the rights of Englishmen does not represent Canadian culture outright. Canadian culture extends beyond official civil culture characterized by tradition and continuity to the experiences on the land which motivated a break with tradition. History represents the official and conservative component of Canadian culture, while geography – traversal and inhabitation of the land – is the place of its disruptive, radical component. This disruption takes the form of a will to independence of identities formed under empire but not of a self-constitution of those identities themselves. It is the experience of the land that is both the disruptive alternative to empire and also the 'progressive' motive for the formation of a new civil culture. While this experience leans on various doctrines available at the time, such as natural rights, its primal character is not dependent on any such doctrine. It is equally, indeed more, drawn to the pre-Enlightenment, ancient doctrine by which the land belongs to those who work it and those who work it belong also to the land – an identity rooted in the inhabitation of a place which empire must necessarily repress. This archaism survives within Canadian political culture even though it is expelled from official culture.

In case it should be supposed that the Métis are the only ones who have asserted this ancient right against the empire and its successor state, let me note the 1910 *Declaration of the Lillooet Tribe*. They state:

> We claim that we are the rightful owners of our tribal territory, and everything pertaining thereto. We have always lived in our country; at no time have we ever deserted it, or left it to others. We have retained it from the invasion of other tribes at the cost of our blood. Our ancestors were in possession of our country centuries before the whites came. It is the same as yesterday when the latter came, and like the day before when the first fur traders came. We are aware that the B.C. government claims our country, like all other Indian territories in B.C.; but we deny their right to it. We never gave it or sold it to them.[6]

Like the Métis, the Lillooet point to their ability to defend their land and to the fact that they never agreed to alienate their sovereignty, but the source of their sovereignty itself resides elsewhere. 'These lands have been continually occupied by us from time out of mind, and have been cultivated by us unmolested for over thirty years.'[7] Again, it is inhabitation, the identity of the people with the land, that confers sovereignty.

It is not my intention to equate the histories of all struggles against empire. There are of course different histories, different struggles, and different strategies. It has been my purpose to isolate within the history of Canada an ancient right to sovereignty that has influenced official Canadian culture but has never been incorporated within it. This ancient right based on inhabitation has been asserted through the different histories of struggle and must be taken seriously by a contemporary critique of empire rooted in this history and culture. Without a concept of inhabitation and the right it confers, to be exercised by a sovereign people not a successor of empire, the critique of empire would remain an imperial critique.[8]

Locality as Subsistence and Sustainability

How can such a right of inhabitation be rediscovered and reinvented in the contemporary world? How can it point beyond particular struggles toward a universalizing defence of inhabitation? If one poses the question of universalization, not from the perspective of the settled universal of empire, but from that of emergent alternatives, the critical, creative role of contemporary movements in defending and redesigning self-reliant and diverse communities can be articulated through the concept of locality. It is about how we will live *here*, how we might inherit and redesign the ancient right of inhabitation. That is the critical moment: when all the global exchanges of empire hover to see whether they will win *here*, whether we will be just another anywhere, or whether this will continue to be our place.

Critical social movements have instituted new sites of struggle and, in this sense, have rediscovered and embraced locality in order to argue against 'homogenization,' 'abstraction,' and 'top-down solutions,' which implies that they anticipate a conception of place that is more than an example, or a case, of a larger plan. The environmental movement has called this 're-inhabitation' and has called for us to live in the world as our home, to live, in Stan Rowe's phrase, in our 'home place,' *here.*[9] There is thus an extraordinary coincidence between environmentalism and the English-Canadian tradition of social and political thought which suggests that the figure of social criticism is reversing in the same way that the English-Canadian tradition reversed the concern for universality to particularity, locality, and here. We no longer need to get beyond, but to 'get back,' to learn to take ourselves and the particularities of our own experiences as the measure of larger institutions and forces. But this cannot be simply a reversal. The experience of place has been shifted by its previous incorporation into abstract universality. Its recovery must also be a peek beyond – but, perhaps not 'beyond' anymore; we need to seek new metaphors here – a 'gearing into,' perhaps, or a 'swaying with,' the places through which we are defined. In short, this new concept of criticism as recovery of place requires a new concept of universalization that does not simply subsume particularity as an example.

The term 'place' has some limitations which can be clarified on the ground of the phenomenology of locality presented in chapter two and that require us to distinguish the term 'place' from 'locality.' Locality focuses on the connection between places, or sites, and is not itself a single site. Even within the environmental movement, where it seems most applicable, the concept of place seems to suggest that there could be an independent republic of Prince George, or of Toronto, whereas such places inevitably require some larger coordination with other places. If independence in the sense of non-connection were the meaning of locality, we would seem to be doomed to rediscover next year the necessity of larger connection and would be stuck with the same forms of administration and institutionalization that have subsumed localities within their plan. Also, if locality is understood to mean a certain area, or place – a here as opposed to a there, the near as opposed to the far – it does not seem applicable to other social movements. The new connection between women that feminism has created is international and not linked to any particular place. Indeed, no movements, not even environmental ones, are restricted to a particular place in this sense. However, what is close, local, to one actor in a social movement is close to other actors as well – wherever they may be in space. Their world is defined through this nearness, rather than through state or corporate organizations, and they anticipate a new world in which this nearness becomes a structuring force, a universalization, in which the world sways to their tune. In this sense, the recovery of place in contemporary terms, which I call 'locality,' is a key feature of all contemporary social movements, about which we should ask: Why have such movements emerged now? What is their meaning?

In the period from the end of the Second World War until its dismantling in recent years, the welfare state achieved a degree of equality and social justice that was unprecedented in North Atlantic capitalist societies. By balancing the endemic inequalities caused by a capitalist economy with redistributive and social security programs enacted through the nation-state, the welfare state managed to bring the working class into the mainstream of capitalist society. The idea of social rights – rights to employment, good working conditions, unemployment insurance, education, health care, pensions, and so forth – that underlay the practice of the welfare state gained the acceptance of a majority of the working class, such that they could see themselves as full, if comparatively powerless, citizens of capitalist society. In return for this inclusion, they accepted the necessity to work and to contribute socially, through taxes, to the maintenance of the society that guaranteed those social rights. T.H. Marshall, the major theorist of the welfare state, explained social rights as 'the whole range from the right to a modicum of economic welfare and security to the right to share to the full in the social heritage and to live the life of a civilized being according to the standards prevailing in the society.'[10] It is important to emphasize in the contemporary context that social rights were universal rights – they applied to everyone equally – and were not simply a 'social safety net' for the poor, unfortunate, or unworthy.

Social rights reformed the capitalist conception of property. The capitalist conception of property is based upon the unrestricted right to exclude all others from the use of a good. Such an exclusive property right had become dominant by displacing an earlier, pre-capitalist conception of property in which various persons and groups could have different property rights in the same thing. Each thing used to be criss-crossed, as it were, by a net of overlapping uses that were recognized in the notion of common property. Common property is the right not to be excluded from the use of a thing, whereas the capitalist conception of property is the right to exclude all others. C.B. Macpherson was referring to this history when he argued that 'the rise of the welfare state has created new forms of property and distributed them widely – all of them being rights to a revenue.'[11] If one has the right not be excluded from a revenue, then one gains the right to exercise one's abilities in the production of that revenue. This right may then be called one's right in a common property. The welfare state made an important incursion into capitalist property by asserting that everyone has a right to make a living and thus that the necessary means for work are common property. This did not mean, of course, that capitalist private property was abolished as such, but rather that the nation-state asserted the right of workers not to be excluded from the provision of jobs by private industry. In short, the state was committed to policies aimed at securing full employment. In Macpherson's words, 'that right amounts to a right of access to the means of labour which they do not own.'[12] A common property in the means to work as enforced by the nation-state was a key component in ending the social marginalization of the working class.

The recognition of social rights and common property in the welfare state forged a new and compelling identity for most members of the working class. These new rights were not simply new elements of their situation but, insofar as the working class identified strongly with them, the identity of the class was itself transformed. They became citizens with rights that extended into the workplace and family. This new identity displaced the us-versus-them mentality that had prevailed previously and brought the majority of citizens to identify with the goals of society as a whole, to create a national moral community that mitigated the competitive individualism and class antagonism of market society.

The welfare state, as a key moment in the history of socialism in which workers became citizens, was characterized by an expanding postwar industrial economy with its emphasis on Fordist production and mass consumption. Expenditures on social rights could thus be combined with an expectation of general employment and a rising standard of living. The basic social unit that was assumed to be the beneficiary of social welfare was the nuclear family. The husband's 'family wage' was complemented by the assumption that the wife would be a full-time mother and housewife.[13] In this sense, the income policies of the welfare state incorporated an institutional separation between social reproduction in industry and in the family that determined the different and complementary relations of men and women. The root of this separation was in the association between women, reproduction, the family, and nature.[14] For these reasons, the ideas and practice of the welfare state should be considered a continuation of the dominant emphasis in the socialist tradition on the idea of progress. Since the eighteenth-century Enlightenment, the idea of progress has been associated with the domination of nature by science and technology such that material wealth for greater general abundance could be created. Such general abundance was believed to provide the essential conditions for a society of greater equality, political participation, and both individual and social development. The socialist tradition differed from the liberal one in arguing that this ideal could only be realized if class inequality were eliminated or, at least, decreased, but the attachment to the idea of moral-political progress through the domination of nature was a common heritage from the Enlightenment.

It is important to note, however, that there was always an important minority tradition that advocated the reconciliation, or harmony, of humanity with nature. The utopian socialists, the early Marx, and the anarchist tradition are the main examples of this tradition. Kropotkin perhaps put the ideal of local self-reliance most clearly when he argued for 'a society where each individual is a producer of both manual and intellectual work; where each able-bodied human being is a worker, and where each worker works in both the field and the industrial workshop; where every aggregation of individuals, large enough to dispose of a certain variety of natural resources – it may be a nation, or rather a region – produces and itself consumes most of its own agricultural and manufactured produce.'[15]

In our time the idea of continuous progress has come under serious criticism, largely due to the nightmarish experiences of the twentieth century in the use of science and technology to intensify the destructiveness of war, repression, and genocide. But it is also apparent that the huge increases in material production during this century have failed to translate into general equality and social participation. The welfare state, being based on the assumption of the idea of progress through industrial growth, has thus been out of step with the major criticism of the idea of progress that has emerged in our time. Moreover, even in the heyday of the welfare state there were factors that suggested that the translation of industrial growth into social equality through national programs entailed some negative effects on social participation and individual development. The institutionalization of social rights through national bureaucracies produced a 'clientism' and de-politicization that reinforced the channelling of expectations into private life defined on a consumerist model. The new citizen-identity as it emerged in the welfare state was thus subject to endemic forces undermining its efficacy from the outset. A contemporary renewal of social rights must take its departure from the evident reality of our time that the expanding Fordist economy on which the welfare state was based cannot be recovered and also that national bureaucracies have a corrosive effect on political life. For these reasons, a contemporary critique of empire must take up the minority tradition, more associated with utopian socialism and anarchism than either social democracy or revolutionary Marxism, which attempted to harmonize humanity with nature and sought human equality and individual development outside of industrial growth. It is not a question of rejecting scientific and technological development, but of rejecting the ideology that such development should be conceptualized as a continuous 'advance,' such that critics are always charged with trying to 'retard' technology or 'return' to an earlier time. The issue is to assert the ethical principles of human equality, individual development, and community as the criteria for what counts as an 'advance' or progress, rather than expecting human goals to simply adjust to developments in science and technology. It is a question of what type of development and for what purposes.

In order to pose the question of how social rights and common property as forms of inhabitation might be reinvented in our time, I want to begin by considering the relationship of the market to the whole range of human activities. Whereas revolutionary socialism attempted to abolish the market, and social democracy has accepted it in its present form, I think that our present task is to consider how to displace, or push aside, the market from its domination of social life through its monopoly over the social representation of value. In this sense, my argument is a later, environmentalist version of the critique of the market elaborated by Marx. While the market may be expected to continue to exist, a central goal of democratic socialism must be that fewer and fewer subsistence needs be obtained through the market and, in general, that the market be subordinated to subsistence needs as defined through a community. A subsistence-oriented economy, unlike a market-driven one, has a decent chance at a sustainable relation to nature. This implies that the legislative activities of national and provincial states, cities, and regions should be oriented toward enabling relatively independent, sustainable communities. (It is important to keep in mind here that 'independent' does not mean separate or isolated, but 'sovereign,' or self-ruling.)

The commodities that are exchanged on the market are defined through their *prices*. Only by having a price does a thing, being, or activity become a commodity. And, through the relation between prices, it becomes essentially comparable to any other commodity. The market is the total system of relative prices and, as such, embodies within itself a system of universal comparability and relative value. In market-intensive capitalist societies, the market is the central form of the social representation of value. You and I as individuals often regard a thing (such as a photograph of a dead friend or relative), a being (such as a human being, a household pet, or a wild goose), or an activity (such as running, growing vegetables, or making love) as having inherent, or *intrinsic value* – that is to say, a value good in itself.[16] But such values are not socially effective; they are 'private' or 'subjective' we say, because they do not enter into the effective social representation of value through the market. If they were to enter into the market by being assigned a price, their value would become socially recognized by becoming a *relative value* in comparison to other things, beings, or activities. It would also raise the issue of how its social value, as represented by its price, has transformed its intrinsic value, the value that inheres in a thing, being, or activity itself.

This poses a problem for environmental issues. If clean water, or a wild goose, *does not have a price*, then its value is regarded as only a private or subjective affair. Thus, environmental issues are often posed in terms of an opposition between objective market value and non-market subjective or emotional values such that environmental concerns are seen as always interfering with, and retarding, the market. They are seen as entirely non-market goods whose only possible effectivity is through state regulation. On the other hand, if environmental goods *are* given prices, they become relative values defined by their price, and, given enough time, one can expect that they will be reckoned less valuable than something else. If a park's value is reckoned by a price, then the condos are not far away.

The monopoly of the social representation of value through the market is thus a general problem for environmental issues. But it is not only environmental issues that are affected in this way. We all perform work that is not valued through a price, or wage. One of the main examples of unpaid labour is domestic work, mainly performed by women, but there is also yard work, fixing the car or children's toys, volunteer community work, shopping, and so forth.[17] While the market system of relative prices is universal in the sense that any thing, being, or activity can be assigned a price, it is in another sense partial. The market *abstracts from* the whole complex of things, beings, and activities that define our practical life. It lifts one aspect out of its practical context and, considering it first in isolation, then sets it into the systemic relation with other aspects that constitutes relative value.

The point is that the market system does not, and cannot, represent the whole of practical life. It necessarily leaves out many things, beings, and activities. More can always be added in, but the process can never be complete. This is because while the market is not extensionally limited – in principle, it can be extended to cover any new commodity – it is limited by the process of abstraction from which it begins. In abstracting from the whole complex of practical life, the market system thus continually raises the question of its applicability and effects in social life as a whole. It is this question that is encapsulated in the distinction between intrinsic value and relative value.

Even in high-intensity market societies, the market relies upon, and affects, a multiplicity of other things, beings, and activities which constitute the fabric of our social lives. The limitations of the social representation of value by the market is thus an important political issue in such societies. One way in which this issue has been posed is in terms of the relation between the market economy and the household in which the situation of women is crucial. Another, as I have already suggested, is in the environmental movement, where the relation between the market economy and natural beings and cycles is crucial. There are, necessarily, many other examples. The argument that I am making in abstract terms refers to all situations in which the relative prices reckoned on the market intersect with the concrete, specific intrinsic values which constitute the quality of our everyday lives in our locality.

A contemporary critique of empire thus requires that the market system be dislodged from its monopoly of the social representation of value. Social economists and critics have coined a number of terms – such as the informal economy, shadow work, or subsistence economy – to refer to transactions that are not represented as prices.[18] I will use the term *subsistence* to refer in the widest sense to all things, beings, and activities in high-intensity market societies that are presupposed by, or ignored by, or outside, the market but that are nevertheless important to the lives of people within such societies. The term subsistence economy is thus a way of formulating the surrounding context within which the market operates and which it continually affects and reorganizes. While the market functions to reorganize subsistence around that which can be given a price, the goal of socialism is to subordinate price, or relative market value, to subsistence.[19]

Subsistence has three main components. One, there are those things, beings, and activities which are necessary to the useful functioning of market-represented values but are not themselves assigned prices. For example, the vegetables that I buy at the corner store have a price, but my buying activity itself does not, nor the walk home, nor the cooking, nor the eating. Two, there are those things, beings, and activities that remain outside the market system. Traditional subsistence, such as growing and eating my own vegetables, would fall into this category as would inherent natural values such as wild geese and clean air. Three, there are those transactions that simply take place outside the market through barter or other informal exchanges. Subsistence represents the practical world defined by the intrinsic values of things, beings, and activities which constitutes the actually experienced form of life, or the qualitative standard of living, of people in high-intensity market societies. The goal of democratic socialism is to increase the qualitative standard of living, or, in the widest sense, the 'real wealth,' of people as experienced in their subsistence.

There are several advantages to thinking in terms of subsistence economy, or practical use-value. It brings into consideration those activities important to the qualitative standard of living – such as cooking, housework, or home repairs and improvements – that are usually invisible. Also, it allows us to reckon what is lost through market exchanges in relation to what is gained. For many people, for example, taking a job to receive a wage requires a long commute to work, frustration in traffic jams, and an expensive car. Some of these costs can be given a price and some cannot, but all must be reckoned against what is gained as a wage. Time lost in a commute that cannot be spent with one's children will never find a price on the market, but it is not hard to understand that it has to do with their quality of life. Finally, the experience of 'need,' in Marx's sense, is rooted in subsistence and can provide the basis for an alternative ethic that can motivate socialist action.[20]

Because of the difference between market values and intrinsic values, market societies have always contained an opposing tendency to the reduction of values to the market. Following Karl Polanyi at this point, I will call such tendencies the 'self-protective response of society.'[21] Such a response comes from those sectors of society who are threatened by market forces. Initially, it was mainly the aristocracy and the working class who enacted measures to limit and contain the market. The vehicle of this response was never confined to the nation-state – the working class's first response, for example, was to form unions – but was mainly institutionalized through regulation of the market by the nation-state. This is because, despite the near-monopoly of the social representation of value by the market, the nation-state became an arena for the articulation and representation of non-market values. The socialist ideal now requires an active dialogue with the new release of energies from contemporary social movements and identities that are proposing non-market values.

Actually existing market societies are thus in tension between two conflicting tendencies. The dominant one tends to reduce all value to relative value represented by a price such that, to put it quickly, if it is not represented by a dollar value, it is not a real, or efficacious, need. A secondary, responsive tendency asserts intrinsic values against the market and looks for alternative forms in which they can be socially represented. The welfare state was one state of relative equilibrium between these two tendencies in which the intrinsic values represented as social rights were effectively asserted through the regulative power of the nation-state. Actually existing market societies are thus riven by a tension between market and community.

The term 'community' refers to those collectivities who have sufficiently asserted intrinsic values against the market to constitute themselves as effective actors in the society. Thus, I do not define communities 'objectively,' or 'structurally,' in terms of their place within the social system. Rather, I define communities by their success at politically articulating a social identity against the exclusions endemic to the social system. A community allows for, and even encourages, a certain degree of internal differentiation. However, it does so against the backdrop of what is asserted as common. In this sense, a social movement not only pursues specific goals but also articulates a social identity which proposes a new commonality. The new commonalities engendered by social movements are the most vibrant current resource for the non-market values, internally differentiated communities, and counter-hegemonic struggles that might reinvigorate the socialist ideal.

My claim is thus that community versus the market, not class versus class, is the main tension of contemporary market societies. And that communities assert themselves as identities, that is to say, as actors who constitute themselves in places where market forces are slack, or have been pushed aside. Such 'places' may be actual places such as neighbourhoods or regions, but the term should be taken more generically. The women's movement operated, in part, through a re-articulation of domestic space and had consequences that could be derived from this re-articulation for public action. While each of these domestic spaces may be separate from the others, there is a metaphorical sense in which the women's movement constituted itself in a strategic 'place' available due both to its relative externality to market forces and to the welfare state assumption of the family wage as norm. Even in the environmental movement – where the tendency to take the 'place' in which social movements operate in the literal, geographically delimited sense of 'place' is strongest – the 'locality' in question is more a principle of connection than of separation, of traversal more than distance. While the tendency of the market is toward uniformity, the protective response is rooted in the re-articulations that occur in slack places, which are of necessity plural, as plural as the threatened intrinsic values which are discovered there.[22]

With the decline of the welfare state, the main community actors have become social movements. Their activism constitutes social identities which resist the relative values promoted by consumer society. The environmental movement, feminism, First Nations movements, urban reform, national and regional movements, gay and lesbian movements, and many more, have been the main forces whereby the market has been held back from entirely dominating society. Their assertion of intrinsic values, subsistence, and concrete experience has forged senses of community that have sustained us and which hold out the promise of renewing the project of democratic socialism. They have done so, by and large, without being able to count on the nation-state for social protection from the market.

The assertion of community by social movements thus provides the basis for assessing the qualitative standard of living of people as experienced in their subsistence that is the goal of democratic socialism. Communities propose new forms of the social representation of value that displace the monopoly of the market. It is in social movements that identities are constructed that become countervailing powers to consumerism and clientism. However, contemporary social movements have been considered primarily as forces that occur outside work and economic production. The main tendency of capitalism has been to reduce necessary work through the introduction of technology and increasingly capital-intensive enterprises; thus it raises the spectre of increasing marginalization for many sectors of the population. And work, in the narrow sense of wage labour, or activity with a price, has become less central to the identity of citizens. But no more now than in the past can socialists consider work that gains a wage on the labour market the criterion of useful activity. If we bear in mind the argument that I have made for displacing the market, and consider work in the wide sense as all useful activity, it can be understood as the crucial link between human beings and nature, as that which transforms nature into a human environment.

It is through human activity that our identities are constructed. Activity that is undertaken in a community brings forth a social representation of its value that makes identity *social* – that puts it into relation with other actors and their activities. When we understand human activity as that which produces subsistence, or concrete well-being, its connection to sustainability becomes clear. Unsustainable practices are tolerated because those who initiate them do not have to live with their consequences. Resources are depleted; natural cycles are violated, for reasons defined outside of a given community. If the profit goes out of the community, the sustainability of the enterprise ceases to be an issue. But communities must live with the consequences of their actions; they have nowhere else to go, unless they simply cease to exist. Thus, economic activity, and markets, become destructive when they cease to be local, that is, based in a community which both reaps the rewards *and* lives with the consequences.

There is thus an important link between the emphasis on locality in sustainable economics and the idea of work as useful activity oriented to subsistence, rather than wage labour. In this way, one can break down the apparent opposition between human action and nature that often appears in environmentalists and anti-environmentalists alike. The prior condition for this synthesis is a critique of the social representation of value by the market and an opening up to new social representations of value in the communities asserted by social movements. The principles and practicality of a sustainable society have been much debated in recent years. Without entering into the details of that debate here, there are two main respects in which the idea of a sustainable society makes an important contribution to contemporary socialism. First, while the idea that human activity can ever be entirely in 'harmony' with nature may well be an over-simplification, it is a definitive break with the Enlightenment idea that greater domination of nature is the vehicle of greater human equality. Posing the issue in terms of a form of human production that is sustainable in the long term in relation to natural cycles and processes entails a break from the ideology of progress that assumes a linear advance or retreat in the domination of nature by science and technology. Second, it then becomes a question of what forms and kinds of human productive use of nature do not destroy their natural basis. Thinking in this way means that both the types of productive relation to nature and their human purposes become amenable to ethico-political evaluation. The idea of sustainable society thus necessarily asserts the priority of ethico-political evaluation over material progress and in this respect returns us to the deeply ethical impulse of socialism from its infatuation with industry.

While it is an important ideal, the idea of a sustainable society as a steady-state relationship between humans and nature has one crucial drawback: to decide that a policy or social arrangement is sustainable in this sense would require an extensive knowledge of natural systems and the impact of social organizations on them. Thus, it would seem to imply that decisions need to be taken by an army of natural and social scientists. Such a high knowledge requirement would undermine democratic participation in decision making. Moreover, even in the apparently optimal case of highly informed decision making by a scientific and technical elite, knowledge is necessarily limited to those studies that have already been done. New impacts on nature by technical innovations, by accumulation of isolated impacts, and by new forms of social organization would still necessarily introduce imbalances into the human–nature relationship. Scientific knowledge of problems necessarily lags behind the identification of those problems themselves. To state it quickly, the knowledge requirement of steady-state sustainability is too high to be realistic and contains an unfortunate undemocratic implication.

But it is not necessary to interpret sustainability in terms of a positive steady-state relationship between humans and nature. The idea of sustainable society arose in the context of an environmentalist critique of many of the practices of industrial society as being *un*sustainable. While sustainability is hard to define, unsustainability is much easier to spot and demands remedial action, if not an ultimate remedy. We should therefore understand sustainability as *not-unsustainability*, a double negation: based in a criticism of unsustainable practices (for which we do have compelling evidence) and as an anticipation of new practices which are, at minimum, less unsustainable than current ones. Such practices will need to be worked out in local contexts in relation to the subsistence of the local population. For this, democratic participation is essential since subsistence wealth, unlike prices, can only be defined by participants.

Human activity in making useful things can thus be made sustainable in relation to nature if the market is displaced from its monopoly on the social representation of value. Democratic participation in local subsistence activities oriented to sustainable practices can provide another form for the social representation of value that might vie with the market to generate new forms of the self-protective response of society. This perspective does not imply that the market needs to be abolished, nor that it needs to be accepted in its current form. It implies that the market needs to be displaced from its monopoly and re-embedded in sustainable, subsistence-oriented practices. In many cases, community and government intervention is necessary to protect local and regional markets from global ones. The right to a revenue, the right to make a living, means the right to participate in the social representation of value. This would be a new form of common property. On this basis, workers, as citizens, could participate fully in the rights and responsibilities of society in a new form by creating spaces for independent community action within the nation-state.

The route to realizing such a subsistence-oriented socialism is itself diverse. Socialism has tended to limit itself to solutions either through the socialization of industry or redistribution by the nation-state. But the diversity of subsistence, articulated through democratic processes that socially represent value, suggests that there is not a single solution to the domination of human activity by the market and its siphoning-off of locally produced value by international money circuits.[23] The goal is to promote and rely upon diverse and interconnected forms of economic activity whose goal is the development of subsistence wealth and useful human activity and that maximize their travel through local circuits and therefore maintain community employment.[24]

It is not likely within the foreseeable future that the global market will subside. I have argued that it is the task for a contemporary critique of empire to build alongside it sustainable, subsistence-oriented local economies that hold out the possibility of withdrawing from dependence on global capital. The transition period will likely be very long, but the task is to build within the shell of the old society the incipient forms of the new and to await the moment when it is demonstrated in the daily lives of citizens that their survival requires a break with the global market.[25]

There may well remain a role for the welfare state – and the assertion of social rights, common property, and community through the nations-state – for the foreseeable future, but the dynamic has now moved elsewhere, and it is a failure if contemporary critical theory allows itself to be limited to a defence of the welfare state. It is only by reconstituting community in new forms, from the ground up, within cooperative forms of self-organization that we can form the social relations that might sustain us in the moment when we are abandoned to environmental ruin and social marginalization by the shiny forces of globalization. These forces will indeed abandon us in the moment when it becomes more profitable to do so. Subsistence and sustainability must be the watchwords of the new critique of empire. Only in this way can we rediscover the possibility of genuine sovereignty through inhabitation.

4 The Principle of Association

Contemporary extension of the critique of empire based in English-Canadian social and political thought has allowed an articulation of the good for humans as local sustainability. This in no way negates a relationship between localities, but rather argues that a universalization must emerge from such relationship instead of being imposed by the a-local, undifferentiated pseudo-universals of empire. Since such an emergent universality repudiates the homogenization of diversity, it must incorporate a positive sense of cultural diversity. I will argue in this chapter that this can be achieved by replacing the model of citizenship confined to the nation-state with a conception of making peace between communities through treaties.

Thinking about diverse identities in the English-speaking tradition normally takes its bearings from John Locke's first *Letter Concerning Toleration* (1689). Well aware of the wars and suffering caused by competing Christian sects, Locke argued for the separation of church and state, of the civil interests of 'life, liberty, health, and indolency of body; and of the possession of outward things, such as money, lands, houses, furniture, and the like' from those of the church in 'the public worshipping of God in such a manner as they judge acceptable to Him, and effectual to the salvation of their souls.'[1] There is no doubt that this separation has been a civilizing influence in societies where it has been adopted and that toleration may still be urged on those receptive to its logic. Locke gives two main reasons for this separation of church and state: one, that toleration 'is so agreeable to the Gospel of Jesus Christ, and to the genuine reason of mankind,' and two, even though there might well be a true church and doctrine of salvation, 'in this great variety of ways which men follow, it is still doubted which is the right one.'[2] The first of these reasons might be mainly rhetorical, in that it is Christians whom he must convince. It is a useful rhetoric insofar as all the Christian sects claim allegiance to the Gospel of Jesus Christ. Locke thus appeals to what is common among the different sects even though it is at the very least a debatable interpretation of the doctrine of that religion. No more is it shown, but only asserted, that 'genuine reason,' or natural reason, philosophy, provides a ground for toleration. Insofar as these count as reasons, and not mere assertions, it is because they are really versions of the second: doubt. It is because of doubt that 'faith only and inward sincerity are the things that procure acceptance with God.'[3] It can with justice be pointed out that this conception of religion partakes in the modern liberation of subjectivity and may even be, for this reason, called Protestant, but this observation does not nullify the appeal that it makes to other conceptions, which would have to reject subjectivity outright to render themselves immune to the appeal that is made in the name of their common allegiance.

I certainly do not want to deny the civilizing effect of the doctrine of tolerance based on doubt about the right sect, but I do want to make an observation concerning its necessarily limited scope. The appeal against the exclusivity of sects is to a higher unity in which all sects partake. Locke does his best to accommodate Jews and Muslims, but he draws the line at atheists. 'Lastly, those are not at all to be tolerated who deny the being of a God. Promises, covenants, and oaths, which are the bonds of human society, can have no hold upon an atheist.'[4] One can appeal from Christian sects upwards to the common umbrella of Christianity, and perhaps appeal from Christianity upwards to the common heritage of the Abrahamic religions of the Book. The logic of doubt about the veracity of a specific sect is that another sect drawing on the same heritage is also credible. Locke's logic is to jump up one level of abstraction, as it were, from a Christian sect to Christianity itself, and strains even above this to include all religions of the Book who bear a filiation to the Hebrew account of revelation. This higher level is what both allows for diversity under its umbrella and defines the limit of toleration in the atheist, who does not fit under the umbrella. If this is the logic of toleration, it is clear that, while it may allow peacemaking in a given context, it is necessarily limited by the shared higher context to which one may appeal. It is a logic of toleration, and not of respect, insofar as one's belonging to a sect and believing with inward sincerity that it is the true one is compatible with tolerating the errors of competing sects if it is the case that the competing sects make appeal to the same sources as one's own. The bottom line is that while one can believe them to be errors, one cannot be certain of it – unless one imagines that the word of God is entirely transparent to humans. A plurality of possible interpretations is allowed by virtue of the appeal to a higher-level belief that, by virtue of being appealed to as the source for tolerance, is put beyond tolerance.

My point here is not that tolerance has limits, which is obvious enough in theory, though often difficult to decide where the limit actually is in political contexts; it is that the higher-level belief is believed in at least as strongly as the sectarian one. Indeed, it must be stronger because it legitimizes a plurality of sects. Thus, while the logic of toleration is civilizing and peace-making within its specific context, it reinforces and stabilizes the common belief at a higher level, often claimed to be universal, and thus draws its limits more sharply.

A post-colonial federalism, or theory of association, is not a theory of tolerance in this sense. It proposes a post-colonial, that is to say, de-centred, political discourse and a plurality of interacting public spheres. Its philosophical core is a conception of universalization as emergent from the interaction of particularities that constitute a tradition rather than a concept of universality that subsumes particulars beneath context-independent rules. The principle of association operative in the alliance between localities can be characterized as a treaty-making protection of particularities. I wish to argue that such a conception is both precedented in English-Canadian culture and philosophy and insufficiently recognized in its official versions. The principle of association for which I argue thus combines appropriation, critique, and proposal in a manner consistent with the procedure of immanent critique that has organized this text. Let us begin, then, with an appropriation of the discourse of federalism in Canada and proceed toward an argument that the inclusion of particularities that this tradition affords can only be adequately defended by extending it toward a multicultural and post-colonial principle of association.

Federalism as Inclusion of Particularities

There are, of course, several strands of interpretation of Canadian federalism. Indeed, I think that Canadian federalism can be regarded as an 'essentially contested concept.'[5] A concept that is contested essentially, rather than solely contested prior to an *in principle* definitive settlement, is a concept whose very meaning depends upon a continuous basic disagreement over its essential features. Such a concept depends upon an 'original exemplar' which is definitive for all parties but whose description can never be neutral between parties. It thus necessarily has a historical dimension. Hannah Arendt's concept of judgment, which she adapted for politics from Kant's aesthetic judgment, was also concerned to isolate features of the use of reason in cases where different views were inevitable and defensible, and could not be resolved by subsuming the particular case under a universal rule. 'Judgment is endowed with a certain specific validity but is never universally valid. Its claims to validity can never extend further than the others in whose place the judging person has put himself for his considerations.'[6] Such judging is a matter of deriving universal considerations from particular examples. In this vein, Kant distinguished between rationalizing and rational judgment. 'We may describe as a rationalizing judgment ... one which proclaims itself as universal, for as such it can serve as the major premise of a syllogism. On the other hand, we can only speak of a judgment as rational ... which is thought as the conclusion of a syllogism, and consequently as grounded *a priori*.'[7] Judgments are then rationalizing or, as we may also say, universalizing when they pertain to the premises from which we begin arguments, rather than to the conclusions toward which we argue. Only conclusions could be rational and universal as such, in the sense that they may, in the optimal case, follow ineluctably from premises, relevant evidence, and the arguments that weld them into coherence. But, when it is a case of describing a historical example in terms that form subsequent arguments and conclusions, a description that rationalizes and universalizes salient features of historical experience cannot be universal without restriction since it devolves back toward selected features of the exemplar that may be argued to have universalizing implications. While an individual exemplar is held to be such by all parties to the controversy, the description of the example is a universalization that can only *appeal* to others through the descriptions, arguments, and evaluations that it makes possible. It can never, not accidentally but in principle, command universal assent and is thus universalizing, but not universal. It expresses and contributes to the rationalizing task of bringing the particularity of our historical embeddedness toward universalizing articulation. Such judgments are thus the crucial process whereby the historical experience of a people both becomes reflexive toward its own history and also proposes a universalization for human reason *tout court* even though its contribution to such human reason remains debatable, a matter for future determination.[8]

Canadian federalism is an essentially contested and universalizing concept of this type, and consequently disagreements about federalism are not only about what the concept means as such but most basically about the meaning of the historical experience of nation-building in Canada and how we want to live in the future. Nonetheless, an essentially contested concept does not bear an open infinity of interpretations. It is shaped and limited by the historical interpretations that have settled upon the exemplar.[9] The original exemplar for Canadian federalism is, of course, Confederation, but further exemplars have been added at crucial moments in its history – such as the inclusion of Newfoundland into Confederation in 1949, the Royal Commission on Bilingualism and Biculturalism, the patriation of the Constitution in 1982, the 1988 Multiculturalism Act, the creation of Nunavut, and the Nisga'a treaty in 2000. These further exemplars, as well as the propriety of including them, are also matters of controversy and serve to highlight features of the original exemplar that may have been previously regarded as of negligible importance.

We may distinguish three main historical interpretations of Canadian federalism. The first, and probably the strongest, is that of Harold Innis and Donald Creighton, which sees Confederation as primarily the creation of a political and economic union by an elite for the purpose of expansion and extraction of resource wealth. Its hero is John A. Macdonald. The strong centralizing tendency of Confederation was seen as a solution to the dissolving tendencies of U.S. federalism. Thus, lamenting the erosion of this concept of federalism, Donald Creighton has claimed that 'Canada has ceased to be the strongly centralized nation which the Fathers of Confederation intended.'[10] The second, and probably weakest, interpretation of Canadian federalism is that harking back to the Reformers, who wanted a U.S.-style compound republic of independent states that delegated powers to a nation-state. This interpretation has not been influential in subsequent history.

It is significant that these two interpretations rest upon the identical presupposition that a nation requires a homogeneous identity for its citizens – whether it is to argue for the creation of a homogeneous national identity or to reject it in favour of regional identities. The lack of a national identity in Canada prior to Confederation meant that the establishment of a strong central and homogenizing state also required the additional power of identity-creation, not merely recognition, and the Canadian nation-state has played this role ever since Confederation. Canadian politics has thus been about identity to a greater extent than other nation-states. This has provoked a complex politics involving the creation and sustaining of national identity; the granting of recognition, or its refusal, to national identities other than pan-Canadian ones, mainly in Quebec and the First Nations; recognition, or its refusal, of sub-national identities by the federal state in policies such as multiculturalism; and the politics of social citizenship and the new identities rooted in social movements that have marked recent years. If one is committed to a strong national, even nationalist, state, the implication is often taken to be that national identity must subsume and even suppress other social identifications. However, if it is possible to accept the legitimacy of a multiplicity of identifications, then the issue rather becomes how they might be harmonized and included within the national context. Such a politics of inclusion is the core of the argument I will make for a post-colonial federalism.

There is a third interpretation of Canadian federalism that abandons the assumption that national association requires a homogeneous identity and seeks to wind together a form of unity through the inclusion of diversities. James Tully calls this 'diverse federalism,' which refers to 'a means of conciliation ... [that] enables peoples mutually to recognise and reach agreement on how to assemble or federate the legal and political differences they wish to continue into the association.'[11] Referring to the role of George-Étienne Cartier in Confederation, Samuel LaSelva points out that 'in the debates of 1865, he noted that opponents of Canadian federation either lamented the existence of racial and local diversities, and thus called for their elimination through a legislative union, *or* appealed to such diversities and particularities in their attempt to discredit any scheme of union, other than a weak confederacy, a defence league, or a free trade area. The implicit issue was homogeneity, and the belief that a nation either presupposed homogeneity or was compelled to create it.'[12]

For this third tradition of Canadian federalism the task was not to pit local particularities against national identity, nor the reverse. To do this, an abstract and homogeneous language of constitutionalism that aims to be culture-blind must be replaced by a constitutional language that incorporates and protects cultural differences. Tully argues that 'if rights were applied without taking these cultural differences into account, the result would not be impartial. The dominant culture would in fact be imposed in each case.'[13] If abstract and homogeneous rules in practice actually reinforce and extend the assumptions of the dominant culture, then diverse federalism requires a different relationship between particular cultural practices and constitutional discourse. LaSelva says 'Federalists are not universalists precisely because they value the particular differences imbedded in local communities and local cultures. But they are not particularists either. The imaginative feat of Federalism is that it uses the complex concept of fraternity to accommodate both the universal and particular within the same state.'[14] Those who are Federalists under this third interpretation refuse the choice between locality and nation and seek to affirm and construct dual, or even plural, overlapping identities pertinent to a plurality of distinct, but not competing, allegiances. Ramsay Cook and J.M.S. Careless have described this as the construction of 'limited identities' in Canada. As Careless has argued, 'the union of 1867 was in large degree a coming together of regions, and so has remained: regions articulated or integrated under a central regime, but surely not reduced or unified thereby.'[15]

A federalism that takes its departure from the legitimacy of varied accommodations of particularities necessarily abandons the notion of a standard set of rules covering all individuals and groups identically and thus poses a basic issue for the concept of equality. It suggests that equality is not to be sought through the imposition of homogeneity but through the recognition of salient differences embedded in particular histories. More accurately, a federalism of limited identities suggests that contemporary politics requires a balance between standardized rules applying to each in the same way and the diverse recognition of particularities. Equality requires not only treating each in the same way, but also, when it is salient, treating each in the manner adequate to the history of their particularity. Thus, the basis for judgment is not primarily recourse to rules, but the recognition that rules are results of historical inclusions and that the primary recourse is to the complex history of the accommodation of particularities. This must include, of course, not only the plurality of differences accommodated but also the plurality of forms of accommodation themselves. Such a federalism rests on the ancient constitution by precedent and its extension through argument that new conditions require the application of precedent to new situations. The complex history of inclusion of differences thus legitimates arguments for the inclusion of new differences and the exploration of new forms of inclusion. Recovering the history of diverse federalism – which has been undertaken by Careless, Cook, Tully, LaSelva, and others – is an important first step, but I think that it is more important to pose the prospective and more radical issue of what form of association corresponds to the possibility of multicultural and post-colonial democracy. Otherwise, it may be assumed that the achieved universality of the Canadian nations-state might substitute for the decentred, emergent universalization required for debate about the form of rule established by empire. It would consider Canadian federalism as an achievement rather than a possibility.

Let us consider some of the factors that need to be taken into account in proposing such an association. First, every person is the home of a multitude of social identities which are called forth in different circumstances. One may be a woman, wife, mother, worker, Latina, Jewish West Coast Canadian without being required to choose among these. The intersections between such identities often bring forth some of the most interesting contemporary politics and arts. One possibility is the centrifugal one. To state it crudely, in a form we have probably all seen, it is to insist that only other such women who are wives, mothers, workers, and so on have enough in common to bear mutual understanding, to suggest that *only* if one shares *all* relevant identifications does one have something in common with another. This insistence indeed necessarily produces fragmentation, and such a centrifugal tendency is certainly strong in contemporary culture. Its apogee would be a general solipsism in which it is asserted that no one can ever understand anyone else – a statement which is truly not worth uttering. This position assumes that particularities are necessarily self-enclosed and incapable of entering into any form of universalization. But there is another possibility, which is that this list of identities produces partial identifications with an indefinite plurality of others. Each identification cleaves one to a different group. Allowing and insisting on the validity of each and all of one's identifications – in a multicultural, plural, and yet interconnected society – asserts one's connections to all others and can constitute a plurality of centripetal forces. Such connections are not of the total person, but of an overlapping kind with indefinite borders. The individual person is thus individual by being the locus of such criss-crossing social identities, not outside them or beneath them.

Second, social movements, when striving for recognition of their particularity, encounter similar claims by others. If I want my Ukrainian ethnic identity recognized, for example, I must recognize and validate the fact that not all other Canadians are Ukrainians. Also, Canadian Ukrainians not only are Ukrainians but have other relevant identities, and thus share a mixed history with other Canadians. In this context, the claim to assert one's ethnic identity becomes a claim for the *right* to maintain ethnic identity, and such a right is a universalization that recognizes the legitimacy of other ethnic identities. Second, in seeking public reform, movements encounter their partiality with respect to other claims within the context of similar critiques of the social system made by other groups. While movements may remain oriented to a single issue, the individuals within such movements are usually drawn to the legitimacy of other claims. This perhaps prefigures an inclusive context in which the inter-relations of both claims may be discussed and addressed. Third, the encounter with other identities can disclose an important plurality within one's own particularity. The environmental movement, for example, has encountered the claim of feminism that men and women have different relations to nature. This has spurred other splinter groups, of course, but it also has enriched the discourse of environmentalism by revealing the social complexity of its issue. Whether it be in discovering the right for the other to be other, in discovering a commonality previously unexpressed, or in discovering an internal plurality in one's claim, the plural context in which identifications occur contains the possibility of a universalization that does not require jettisoning particularities. The new identities that have emerged in recent years pose the question of how they can be included within federalism in order to counter the logic of devolution.

All four of these factors promoting universalizations through the recognition of particularities depend upon the existence of a *context of interaction*. It is the revitalization of this context of interaction that is most significant for a new federalism designed to accommodate the particularities of the heretofore excluded. The diverse federalism of limited identities has been the historical interpretation that has most incorporated particularities. It is thanks to the precedent and effectiveness of this view of federalism that a public context exists which serves to reduce the centrifugal tendency toward fragmentation. To speak comparatively: where a federalism of delegated powers predominates (such as in the United States), or an elite economic management (such as Britain or France), the tendency toward fragmentation will be much stronger. To the extent that particularities are genuinely included into a larger federalism, the remaining institutions expressing cultural particularity become partial institutions within the federal context rather than institutions competing for sovereignty. It is certainly not the case that the existing Canadian Federal state constitutes such a genuinely post-colonial and multicultural universalization. My argument is that the interpretation of Canadian federalism as the inclusion of particularities has historical precedent, but it is only partially achieved. Recognition of the legitimacy of this (third) interpretation by a number of contemporary authors is a key first step that would strengthen the rights of particularities. My own argument is for the radicalization of the notion of including particularities through a focus on their common context that grounds a concept of universalization. Such a concept would overturn entirely the historical force of the nations-state in subsuming particularities and ground a new post-colonial and multicultural universalization. It is thus a matter for political philosophy, not political science, or description. While grounded in a history, it takes that history as a point of departure, not of arrival.

The same principle would apply to the Canadian nations-state as well within the international context. To the extent that Canadian particularity was taken up into a world federation, national sovereignty could be ceded.[16] This is, in my view, a key advantage of my radicalization of the third interpretation of Canadian federalism: it does not even take the institution of the Canadian nations-state as a basic assumption and can conceive of conditions under which it would be reasonable for a Canadian to abandon it. Unless one can so conceive, one's idea of national identity functions as a barrier to human universality, not as a springboard toward it.

If a renewed federalism presupposes a critique of colonialism, as I am suggesting, then clearly it must align itself with those who have called for understanding Canada as a nations-state (in the plural) composed of three main groups: English Canada, by which I mean the multicultural polity whose public language is English; Quebec, by which I mean the multicultural polity whose public language is French; and the First Nations, which include the many nations existing prior to European contact as they have evolved up to this day.[17] These three involve distinct formations and issues because they are positioned differently with regard to the colonial legacy. Federalism can only genuinely be renewed to the extent that it rids itself of the legacy of conquest. The creation of Nunavut and the Nisga'a Treaty shows that this is a difficult, but not impossible, task. The account of Louis Riel in the previous chapter serves to indicate that empire has ruled, and continues to rule, by allowing official recognition of sub-national identities at the price of ceding the right to self-rule.

The continuing weight of the legacy of conquest has determined the superficiality of government attempts at inclusion of Aboriginal nations and Quebec. Without genuine inclusion, which means renouncing the colonial legacy, the national aspirations of these groups have become centrifugal forces fragmenting the Canadian nations-state. That inclusion of Quebec has not been genuine I take to be demonstrated from the breaking of the convention of unanimity among provinces in passing the Constitution Act (1982) and by the pervasive fact that in English Canada any rights ceded to Quebec are taken to be rights of provinces (not of a people) and thus to be imitated by the other provinces. This has affected English-speaking Canada as well, which has suffered the muting and frustration of its collective consciousness by its failure to conceive of itself as a distinct people, and the disintegration of its capacity to act at the Federal level. But the number three in the current formulation of the Canadian nations-state is a passing phenomenon. It is self-rule that is at issue, not the number of official groups. In this sense, it is the remaining still-dissident group that is more important than whatever number of officially recognized identities.

A Post-Colonial Principle of Federalism

While I have argued that a form of federal association based upon an alliance, or the inclusion of particularities, is an important, though not unchallenged, basis of Canadian federalism, I do not mean to suggest that it has been adequately fulfilled in the contemporary nations-state. In fact, my argument is that a clear recognition of this precedent would take federalism beyond the legacy of empire toward a multicultural and post-colonial principle of association. Moreover, while I have, in accordance with the emphasis of Canadian history, focused on ethnic groups as the important case of sub-national identities, I intend this discussion to be pertinent to cultural identities in general. Such a conception is not unprecedented throughout the world. One important precedent is in the federalism of the neglected nineteenth-century political thinker Pierre-Joseph Proudhon.

A politics of alliance refers to the relation between constituted groups and does not inquire into the processes or principles of their formation. The individual, or person, can be a member of more than one group. It is the cross-membership, or multiple identity, that constitutes the 'person' who is involved in the politics of the new alliance proposed by social movements. The international, or post-national, 'person' is a member of a plurality of communities, each of which embraces different principles of internal association and pursues different purposes. This implies a redefinition of the 'person' as the intersection between a plurality of communities, not as a liberal 'individual' constituted outside community and only subsequently, and instrumentally, entering into it. This plurality of intersecting communities overcomes the closed character of traditional communities and insists de facto that communities adapt themselves to the possibility that their members may leave, which functions to strengthen the rights of participation within communities. The post-national person thus can postulate the importance of 'community' as such to human life, independent of a specific community, which raises the question of the recovery of 'belonging' in a new form.

The principle of association that is emerging between groups in the alliance against the globalization of free trade does not address the internal constitution of the groups themselves but is oriented rather to the 'external' conditions for alliance between differently constituted groups.[18] Particular groups form an alliance without subsuming their particularity into the alliance by using what we might call a 'neo-Proudhonian' conception of federation as the basis for free association. Here is Proudhon's definition:

> *Federation* from the Latin *foedus*, gen. *foederis*, that is to say, pact, contract, treaty, convention, alliance, etc., is an agreement by which one or several heads of a family, one or several communes, one or several groups of communes or states, bind themselves by mutual and equal agreements for one or several determinate aims, for which the responsibility falls specifically and exclusively on the members of the federation. The contracting parties ... not only bind themselves ... they assure themselves individually more rights, liberty, authority, and property than they give up ... Any agreement ... that demands the associates' total effort deprives them of their independence and forces them to devote themselves solely to the association.[19]

We may note that the question of the internal organization of the group is not addressed at all by Proudhon in this context, implying that this is not a matter for regulation. Also, it is important that federation is for a determinate or delimited goal, such that the organization remains distinct and is not merged into a larger association. For this reason, Proudhon's concept of federalism seems closer to the idea of an alliance, rather than what we normally think of as a federation, or confederation. The constituent groups retain their particularity because the alliance is for temporary and limited purposes. The alliance remains permanently tentative and must court the agreement of the constituent groups by appealing to the reasons that each particularity has for entering an alliance. Thus, the alliance cannot become a power *over* the constituent groups.

A treaty can be accepted by both sides, but in different terms based on their internal understanding of it. As Joseph Gosnell, President of the Nisga'a Tribal Council, said in his speech on the Nisga'a treaty to the British Columbia legislature, 'What is it about a treaty? To us, a treaty is a sacred instrument. It represents an understanding between distinct cultures and shows respect for each other's way of life.'[20] There are no rules, other than respecting a promise, for treaties, only a history open to a plurality of interpretations. This gives rise to a common history shared by the treaty-making groups that is constituted by the necessary plurality, not only of different interpretations, but of different conceptions of interpretation themselves. Treaties imply a politics of peacemaking based upon mutual respect. Such respect is not founded on knowledge of the other, but on the history and ethics of interaction with other traditions.

A more difficult question would be when, and how, the alliance could expel a group. This limit would be reached when a given constituent group, either through its internal actions on its own members or by external actions, broke decisively with the mutual understanding upon which the alliance depended. It seems clear that the internal actions of a given group, insofar as we restrict ourselves here to the principle of alliance itself, must be largely, or even entirely, outside the jurisdiction of the alliance. With regard to actions oriented outside the group, such actions must clearly not contradict the mutual understanding of the alliance – though it need not necessarily further them. Being an autonomous group, which allies with other groups for limited purposes, a given group clearly reserves to itself the right to have purposes different from the alliance on the sole condition that they do not contradict those of the alliance. There is clearly room for a great deal of debate as to whether different actions are contradictory to the general purpose or not. One of the main politics of alliance will concern the extent to which other, heterogeneous purposes of other groups are merely different or should be seen as contradictory.

What are the 'determinate aims' (to use Proudhon's phrase) of the anti-imperial, anti–free-trade alliance that is legitimated by a new politics of inhabitation? I have argued that, in general, the commonality in question is the defence of various particular forms of community, especially those constructed by, and within, social movements. More specifically, recent observers have defined the alliances that activate what they call 'globalization from below' as the 'violation of widely accepted norms.' 'When widely accepted norms are violated, it can cause concern in many quarters, including both those directly affected and other people who believe in the violated norms. A network of those concerned may form or an existing network may take up the issue.'[21] This observation – in a manner similar to the principle of alliance which does not ask about the internal constitution of groups – does not address the origin or legitimation of norms. It assumes norms to be already existent and with some social force and points out that it is their violation that is a galvanizing component of the alliance between groups. The determinate aims of the alliance are thus rooted in widely shared ethical norms and an analysis of the fundamental processes by which they are being systematically violated. The principle of alliance is the defence of such particularities but not their subsumption under a genus – such as the nation-state – that would render them comparable as instances of a case. It is this desire to resist subsumption that I have found common to the new social movements active on a world scale and a federalism of particularity rooted in the aspirations of ethnic groups in Canada. Its legitimation as a political goal depends on the land-based critique of empire in English Canada in dialogue with other political traditions that aim at a form of association that is not a subsumption of particularities.

Cultural Diversity as a Component of National Identity

The plurality, diversity, and mixing of cultural traditions is a feature of life in the early twenty-first century which can be expected to continue and accelerate. In Canada, thinking concerning cultural plurality and diversity has been generated by multiculturalism, and it is here that thinking concerning the implications of cultural plurality can begin. By multiculturalism I mean mainly the public legitimation of the daily practice of interaction between distinct cultural groups, and only secondarily the policy or theoretical formulations that have attempted to understand this practice.

The most common objection to multiculturalism is that it fragments the nation, which supposes that ethno-cultural allegiances *compete with* allegiance to the nation-state. Critics of multiculturalism suggest that we should all be just Canadians – that we should focus on what unites us, not what divides us. This is also true of critics of multiculturalism in Australia, Argentina, and, indeed, probably everywhere. Multiculturalism is seen as a policy of division which competes with national identity. Equality, it is claimed, consists in all citizens, considered individually, being treated similarly, which means that sub-national communities are ruled out of the public democratic process (and treated only as voluntary organizations of individuals).

Let us look at this criticism a bit more closely. For ethnic identity to compete with national identity it must refer to the same domain of relevance. It is possible for me to be a husband and father, for example, and still to be a Canadian. As identifications, or cultural identities, they do not compete. As even critics of multiculturalism would acknowledge, I can be born in England and be a Canadian – as someone else can be born in Japan and be Canadian. And, of course, one can be born in Canada within a family that has ties to another country because of emigration by one's ancestors.[22] Thus, ethnic identification and a national one do not *necessarily* conflict. It is the multicultural promotion of ethno-cultural identification that is claimed to conflict with national identity, say the critics. It is supposed that *either* one identifies with a group that is defined by its *difference* from other Canadians *or* one identifies with what we all have in common. Thus, a polarization has been set up – *either* national identity *or* multiculturalism – such that it is almost impossible to argue for multiculturalism and national identity simultaneously. Yet that is the argument that I will make. In so doing, I attempt to provide a justification for multiculturalism that pertains to its application as a key component of democracy for the conditions of cultural diversity which will predominate in the twenty-first century.

To get around this unfortunate polarization, the issue can be better defined in this way: 'How can ethno-cultural identity be understood as a *key content* of national identity?' In order for one to experience his or her ethno-cultural belonging as not competing with his or her national identity, it must be seen as a component of national identity. That is, national identity is *experienced in a certain way through the specific ethno-cultural identification*. Most descriptions of the multicultural encounter fail to capture it and reduce multiculturalism to intercultural encounter by describing it as an us–them relationship. In contrast, I argue that the multicultural encounter should be understood as an us–we relationship. That is, as a member of an ethno-cultural group one is a member of an 'us' that is different from others, but as a member of a multicultural society one is a member of a 'we' that includes both the 'us' and also other similar 'us' groups of which one is not a member. Instead of posing the issue as a question of belonging to one constituted collectivity versus another – which implies that they are within the same domain of relevance – it should be posed as two levels of identification for the same individual – one level at which my membership in an ethno-cultural group defines my *difference* from other groups within the nation-state and another level at which my *common* membership in the national group which I share with others of different ethnic groups *allows for and validates* my membership in a specific group. Ethno-cultural belonging is a *way in which* one participates in nationality. So defined, multiculturalism is an interplay of identity and difference and not a choice between them. Multiculturalism understood in this way sets up a unique relationship between the particular aspects of ethno-cultural belonging and the shared aspects of national identity such that the right to ethno-cultural belonging can be sustained as a universal right.

Until recent years, the Canadian nation-, or nations-, state provided a hegemonic framework within which the relationships between culture, economy, and politics were stabilized. A relatively homogeneous national political culture combined with a significant role for national politics in economic development allowed the nation-state to partition and harmonize cultural concerns. Cultural differences were seen as a matter for familial relations or voluntary (ethnic, artistic) organizations, on the one hand, or as driven by the requisites of work and commerce on the other. This division was held together by a dominant national culture assumed to be equally shared by all citizens that could therefore be presupposed in political decisions. This retrospective view is, of course, an ideal type and perhaps even a caricature, but it may provide a useful background for clarifying the shifting boundaries and new issues we face today. National cultures can no longer be seen as equally shared by all citizens. Therefore national cultures must now be thematized in their relations to minority cultures within the nations-state and to emergent (often international) cultural formations brought into being by social movements.

Culture is a concept which necessarily implies a plural in the sense that one's own culture would be invisible as such unless it were to encounter another culture. The us–them formulation is thus built into the instituting moment of the concept of culture. It corresponds to the moment of the discovery of the concept through going out from one's own culture and encountering another. Another way of living that initially might seem merely nonsensical, or even not quite human (and thereby understood through the contrast of civilization with barbarism, or savagery), is grasped as *another* culture when its internal sense is discovered. It is from this instituting moment of travel, or intercultural communication (perhaps clearest in the imperial origins of anthropology), that the notion of culture as an enclosed and internally coherent way of life has developed. There are two main responses to this discovery of an alien culture: The alien culture can be denigrated as less human, or less civilized, issuing in the hierarchical relation characteristic of colonialism. Also, it can reflexively generate a conception of the specificity of one's own culture, in contrast to the other, and one might come to see one's own activities, thoughts, and beliefs as enveloped within a cultural form. While the concept of culture at this instituting stage of its development suggests that culture is a self-enclosed vessel, nevertheless the condition for the emergence of the concept of culture is that cultures do indeed interact and that a relation between them – often, though not always, a colonial hierarchical one – is established.

In our own time – characterized by world-wide immigration, international cultural industries, ethnic violence, and the decline of the nation-state – the concept of culture developed from this instituting moment is no longer adequate. Indeed, it often tends to reinforce exclusivist and colonial tendencies. A contemporary concept of culture must thus take its departure from a critique of the basic components of this first-level concept: (1) the idea of intercultural communication, or contact, as accomplished through travel, or movement between cultures already subsisting independently; (2) the idea of culture as an enclosed vessel based on an internal–external duality, where one is either inside or outside; and (3) the consequent notion of cultural contact as a relation between 'us' and 'them' groups. A contemporary concept of culture would thus take its departure from three basic ideas: (1) the identities of cultures are formed, and exist as such, through their inter-relation – through an encounter with their limits; (2) the cultural condition is, from the first, multicultural – that is to say, characterized by the interplay of diverse cultures; and (3) cultural interchange consequently is, or ought to be, understood to occur between 'us' and 'we' groups.

The multicultural context is characterized by the interaction between ethno-cultural groups such that it produces a context of justification that applies to each of the plurality of groups and demands of each group that it recognize the legitimacy of other groups by means of providing a justification *in its own terms* for the multicultural context. Since the justification of a common context is made in many terms, each belonging to a particular culture, the common context is not an overarching context-independent universality which subsumes particular cultures, but a different sort of identity altogether that can be called a universalization. The archaic and exclusivist aspects of ethnicity that have recently resurfaced in ethnic nationalism are removed by a multicultural civic context which puts ethnic belonging into a universalizing discourse. The multicultural context is not just a context of a plurality of cultures; it is a context of *interaction between cultures* in which legitimation points in two directions: back, as it were, to legitimate particularity – or the relevance of ethno-cultural belonging in a public context – and forward to propose a universalizing claim that requires critical translation into other cultures. The multicultural context thus requires that public speech embody both a defence of one's own particularity and a universalizing claim to the defence of particularity as such.

While multicultural society is, in an obvious sense, the context for particular ethno-cultural traditions, it is important to note that the reverse may also be the case. Particular ethno-cultural traditions are also the context for the legitimation of multicultural society. This point may be explained succinctly with reference to speech act theory. The concept of a speech act, as explained by J.L. Austin, refers to statements which do not describe an action, or state something about an action, but rather *perform*, or actually *do*, the action itself.[23] A classic example of a performative statement is 'I now pronounce you husband and wife.' Considering speech as action has the advantage of shifting attention from the internal truth or falsity of a statement towards what is done, or accomplished, by the statement. To consider language mainly in its performative dimension brings into focus the whole range of issues that have been traditionally classed as problems of rhetoric rather than dialectic, issues of persuasion rather than truth. My interest is not in the classification of statements as such but in the role of public speech acts in conditions of cultural diversity.

The multicultural speech act embodies a relation between content and context in which the two terms may shift such that either may become context for the other. Generally speaking, we may say that such a situation arises when a reflexive statement cannot be stabilized by a hierarchization of levels of discourse. Self-reference takes a paradoxical form in the absence of an established hierarchy of meaning. An ethical claim, since it is made from within a cultural tradition, always involves two levels of meaning. In the multicultural context, no cultural tradition can claim unquestioned legitimation; thus the relation between statement and tradition cannot be definitively hierarchized. The speech act thus comes to encompass the two levels of meaning in a reflexive relationship. Since the claim is made in a multicultural context, it cannot be stabilized as subordinate to the cultural tradition from which it emerged. It may thus become the context for judging the cultural tradition itself. For example, a tradition that is capable of legitimating a strong claim to individual rights may motivate the respect of other traditions and may influence them to develop those aspects of their tradition that tend in this direction.

We may thus refer to the *multicultural speech act* in order to explain the way in which an utterance and the field of discourse within which it normally takes on meaning may shift their relationship. Such a paradoxical relationship brings a tradition of thought into question in the context of a specific debate. The multiculturalism of the multicultural speech act consists in the interconnected plurality of traditions of legitimation within which a given speech act makes sense and takes effect. The plurality of traditions of legitimation has the consequence that a given act no longer is straightforwardly dependent, as it were, on the discursive context provided by a tradition. A given act can also become the site for a critical interrogation of a tradition as a whole, since it does not depend on a single tradition for its meaning and effect, but upon a multicultural context constituted by the inter-relation and mutual translation of traditions.

In order to do this, the concept of multiculturalism must be expanded to include the somewhat distinct notion of a *post-colonial* speech act in order to clarify a certain component of the plurality of legitimating traditions. This plurality – which has been present in Canada since its colonial inception and has, at least to some degree, always found official recognition – can be domesticated through the colonial assumption that one discourse is the only *legitimate* basis for the adjudication of competing claims. The post-coloniality of a speech act thus consists in the recognition that the plurality of traditions is legitimate. It therefore legitimates a plurality of traditions to which a speech act may refer to provide a meaningful context in intervening in public discourse. Post-coloniality thus refers to the impossibility of hierarchizing the plurality of traditions.

A discourse can be said to be multicultural insofar as the cultural tradition upon which a given speech act draws for its legitimation is not the only relevant cultural tradition upon which a responding speech act can draw. A discourse can be said to be post-colonial insofar as the institutional tradition within which a speech act occurs is open to debate about the rules on which it is based, not only the practices that refer to the rules. Within such a discourse one must address not only the question of 'the right of the other to speak' but also the question of the 'legitimate tradition(s)' within which such speech will be interpreted. Aboriginal speech, for example, has been present in Canada since its inception, but the Canadian nations-state has never ceded it an equal right of interpretation because it has never been able to define the rule of interaction between cultural groups. The law, for example, has always been monopolized by the empire and its successors. Speech that is barred from touching the rules of interaction becomes a 'minority' speech precisely through this bar. It is relegated to being a content, whereas imperial speech not only provided content but also a rule which decided the manner of interpretation of the speech act in question. In principle, post-coloniality thus refers not only to the presence of a plurality of traditions in a given context but primarily to the inability of any one of these traditions to monopolize the rules. If no single tradition 'owns' the context, then every speech act functions in a double fashion: as a statement in a given debate and as a 'representative' of the tradition which gives it meaning, such that this representation constitutes a claim to interpret the context of interaction.

The multicultural and post-colonial subject is thus constituted by two 'levels' of identifications. Instead of identifying directly with the nation, the subject identifies with a sub-national group such as a linguistic, ethnic, gender, social movement, or regional identity, and *through this identification* identifies also *in a particular way* with the nation. The nation is thus constituted by its internal diversity. The political subject is consequently in an us–we relation with other groups, not an us–them relation.

The Minority Bar

There has been a plurality of cultural traditions in Canada since its colonial inception which has, at least to some degree, always found official recognition. However, such plurality can be domesticated through the colonial assumption that one discourse is the only *legitimate* basis for the adjudication of competing claims. The critique of empire sketched in the preceding chapter implies a post-colonial politics that consists in the recognition that the plurality of traditions is legitimate. Therefore, there must be a plurality of traditions to which one may refer to provide a meaningful context for an intervention into public discourse. Post-coloniality thus refers to the impossibility of hierarchizing the plurality of traditions.

I have defended a certain interpretation of federalism as the history of (themselves diverse) processes of inclusion of particularities into a proposed universalization – though I have admitted that this interpretation has never been clear enough, even to itself, due to the imperial legacy. Thus, federalism should be understood as a tradition of diverse accommodations rather than submission under a homogeneous set of institutional arrangements. The centring legacy of Canadian federalism due to its origin in the British Empire, with its continuing imperial relation to internal nationalities through conquest, has been displaced – though certainly not overcome – through the history of specific acts of accommodation to particularities. Empire allows the other to speak but controls the rules of interaction between speakers such that the context, or the rules of interaction, is itself monopolized. The radical democracy implied by a critique of empire therefore contains an emergent concept of federation that must address not only the question of 'the right of the other to speak' but also the question of the 'legitimate tradition(s)' within which such speech will be interpreted. Aboriginal speech, for example, has been present in Canada since its inception, but has never rivalled the Canadian nation-state in establishing the rules. Speech that is barred from touching the rules of interaction becomes a 'minority' speech precisely through this bar. It is relegated to being a content, whereas imperial speech not only provided content but also invoked a tradition which decided the definitive interpretation of the speech in question. In principle, post-coloniality thus refers not only to the presence of a plurality of traditions in a given context but primarily to the inability of any one of these traditions to monopolize the rules. If no single tradition 'owns' the context, then every public speech act functions in a double fashion: as a statement in a given debate and as a 'representative' of the tradition which gives it meaning, such that this representation constitutes a claim to establish the rule of interaction.

There are three possible models of the relation between a particularity and the common context, each depending upon the formulation of a self–other relationship. Model one refers to a self–other relation in which the rule is established by one of the parties, thus dominating the context: in this case, the self addresses the other as the one who owns the rules of discourse within which the self–other relation takes place. This is an imperial and colonial relationship of domination. The other is inside by being subject to the rule but outside by dint of being incapable of establishing the rule. Model two refers to a self–other relationship in which the commonness of the context of interaction remains unquestioned, unexamined, and thereby functions as a universal rule which subsumes particularities. This often occurs when the imperial rule or context is taken to be obviously unsurpassable because it has become common sense as a continuation and normalization of the situation of model one. The imperial relationship is operative to the extent that failing to address the rule that defines the context allows the description of the self–other relation to become an apology for empire by erasing the history of its extension over others. In this sense, the other is inside the imperial space in the same manner as the self at the price of relinquishing what is distinctive about its cultural identity. Whereas in the second case the other is taken to be already within the imperial space, and thus not significantly other at all, in the first case the other's difference cannot be avoided but is hierarchized under rules defined by the empire. Scotland, for example, resisted imperial rule with some efficacy up to the Battle of Culloden (1746) but then moved from the first case into the second. Dominated by empire, the Scots – at least most of them – were brought to share its assumptions. The same fate has been visited upon the Métis. Of course, these models compress a great deal of history and struggle against incorporation and underplay the extent to which this process is incomplete and the dream of independence survives in unofficial culture. I have attempted to suggest that we are now in a time in which the imperial legacy that was taken over into the nation-state, then nations-state, has begun to unravel such that the dream of self-rule can be dreamed again. Model three, a genuine concept of a self–other relation, must address the imperial rule that defines the context within which this dialectic has historically been confined. The critique of empire is thus the condition for the relation of self and other to itself constitute the rule or context of interaction. The rule would be amenable to no other legitimation than that worked out through the history of the self–other relation itself. This would be a post-colonial, post-imperial conception of a substantive public good encompassing diverse cultural traditions. My argument suggests that by bringing to light and criticizing the presumption of empire to define the rule of interaction, one may promote a more genuine self–other relation between communities which defends the particularities of their cultural identities. This is the task of a contemporary English-Canadian political thought that strives to articulate the hope embedded in the structuring conditions of Canadian culture and history. A relationship of this sort has been understood since classical times, not under the figure of tolerance, but under that of friendship.[24] One is different from a friend, and does not expect complete agreement, but wishes to allow the friend to prosper and to maintain connection. The political expression of friendship is the treaty. Taken to its limit, it implies a politics of treaty and of peace rather than a politics of citizenship under the umbrella of the nation-state. This emergent politics is reflected in critical social movements and implies a solidarity with their projects of displacing neo-liberal globalization with another 'order' whose outlines are emerging, but yet dimly. To fulfill its promise, such an order would open the possibility of a future of peace and treaty where it is not our sameness but rather our difference that grounds association. Critique of empire and a politics of locality are the herald of this future. This is the content for the human good without restriction that can be recovered, extended, and universalized from the distinctive identity of English Canada.

Empire rules. Empire makes the rules – not only empire understood as an external force but also as it has been inherited by the Canadian nations-state that was constructed by empire and has exercised an internal imperial force within Canada. It rules by making the rules. Any part remains a part precisely because it must petition those who make the rules. The rule makers claim universality precisely because they need not petition. Those who speak the language of those who need not petition, whether within Canada or without, speak the language of empire. It is this language that establishes the common locus which rounds the parts out into the tame self–other dialectic that has dominated our official culture. Its function is to keep the parts as parts, to dampen their claim to judge and not have to petition, to rule themselves. Self-rule is the emergent dream of the periphery, a dream that must be dampened by the centre, with the redcoats, if necessary. The right of such self-rule is the ancient right of inhabitation. Independence, however, could not mean isolation in the space-traversed culture of the periphery. It must mean independence among others, a plurality of independences, a new federation.

It is Louis Riel and the two North-West Rebellions that perhaps most clearly raise the question of the radical outside of empire to which the critical thinker must attend. Their remarkable and little-known *Declaration* of self-rule shows the claim of the periphery to become innovative and independent, to undermine the claim of the empire to provide the rules for negotiation between parts. Their self-foundation revealed the partiality of the empire's rules; it revealed the proposed universality of their self-given and self-limiting rules. It embodies the dream of independence that the New World proposed at the limit of Europe's empires. It punctuates the superficial claim that Canada is the most European, or social-democratic, New World nations-state and reveals the critical polarity between modern and archaic that defines Canadian culture: the most archaic, that inhabitation of the land confers the right to self-rule.

The distinction between the situation of French-speaking Québécois – who claim a seat in discussions of federalism as the representative of a people – and of Ukrainian-speaking Albertans – who can claim only to be one group in a multicultural society – is not one of principle, but is historical. It depends upon the extent to which, or manner in which, one's particularity has been included. Once in, one becomes a member of a subcultural nation or group in a multicultural society. Left out, one is a member of a separate nation aspiring to sovereignty. The line between in and out is defined by the historical struggle for inclusion and the degree of its success – what we might also call the critique of colonialism. Thus, the three nations now predominant may be different, more or less in the past or future. The key component for such a historical interpretation is the extent to which each party is, or has been, accepted as capable of co-determining the rules of the context of interaction.

Dominating the history of interaction between Euro-Canadians and Aboriginal people has been the deep-rooted assumption that Native people are subject to, in Noel Dyck's term, 'tutelage' by Euro-Canadians. Tutelage refers to 'a form of restraint or care exercised by one party over another as well as the condition of being subjected to such protection or guardianship. ... The tutelage that Canadian Indians have experienced has been based neither on a contractual agreement nor a negotiated understanding but upon the power of one side to regulate the behaviour of the other in accordance with a set of unilaterally selected purposes.'[25] Only the abandonment of tutelage – that is to say, an assumption of adult capacity and authority by both parties – can render the process of inclusion a genuine one. Such an assumption of sovereignty by each party decentres the rules by which accommodation is made. The rules become open to negotiation as well. The legitimation of any agreement will be accepted by both sides, but in different terms depending on the internal cultural and political resources for interpreting it. Moreover, such resources become shared in the act of agreement, so that each side gains a cultural-political resource for future interpretations, even though it does not inhabit them in the same way as the other group. It is the colonial legacy that has deformed this potential of an inclusive and decentred federalism. Tutelage is, at its most basic, the claim to monologically dominate the rules of interaction.

If we imagine the future form of a politics that has minimized the colonial legacy, it can be defined through a new form of public speaking that can be called the post-colonial speech act. I have argued that being 'let in' to an inclusive federalism requires both retention of particularities of the way of life of sub-national groups and also a context of interaction between these particularities that allows for universalizing claims. Such claims are politically significant for the reform and foundation of institutions that solidify and extend the context of interaction. There is thus a key relationship between the universalizing context and the plurality of different particular contents. As long as Canadian federalism remains hooked to the colonial legacy, the context of interaction remains fixed at the level of the nations-state and its traditional institutions. In fact, the context of interaction is, in this case, identical with the institutions of the nations-state, and the relations between the national elite and marginalized groups are stratified as forms of tutelage. However, if the critique of colonialism is pushed to its logical conclusion, the context of interaction becomes the basis for a critique and de-centring of traditional institutions – which sets up a new relationship between the context and its particular contents such that they can reverse their roles. A key symbolic affirmation of such a post-colonial federalism would be to remove any reference to the monarchy from Canadian Federal institutions.

It is easy to see how and why the different particularities of a plurality of ways of life can be the content for their context of interaction. However, as the centring legacy of colonialism recedes, the context of interaction can increasingly be defined only in the terms of the particularities included into a renewed federalism. The universalizing context of interaction is legitimated in a plurality of different ways by the particularities that have been included. In other words, each included particularity can become the context for assessment of universalizing claims. A post-colonial federalism can thus be defined as one in which the relation between context and content is reversible between particularities and universalizing claims. Or, to say it somewhat differently, that each way of life included within federalism becomes a context in which the claims of federalism can be evaluated. Such a situation in which context and content are reversible emerges when a reflexive statement cannot be stabilized by a hierarchization of levels of discourse. Colonialism necessarily rests on tutelage insofar as tutelage is the attempt to hierarchize the relationship between content and context by monopolizing the design of rules of interaction. When empire defines the degree of inclusion of a cultural particularity, such particularity becomes a minority within a subsuming universality. It is the barring of particularity from defining a common universalization that constitutes its subsumption. The continued, though often veiled, rule of empire thus proceeds through this 'minority bar.'

Every ethico-political claim is made from within a cultural tradition and therefore includes two levels of meaning. Usually, the tradition provides the context for the content of the particular claim. Clearly, the federal context of interaction provides a context for particular traditions. However, in the context of a de-centred plurality of cultural traditions, every ethico-political claim can also be judged from within each particular tradition. Thus, particularities provide the context for evaluation of universalizing claims that span particularities. At this point, we witness the emergence of the post-colonial speech act in which the relation between particularities and universalizations is such that either can provide the context for the other. The meaning of an individual claim is thus constitutively paradoxical insofar as context and claim become mutually defining and reversible. Speech in such a de-centred situation requires a cultural tradition to define its meaning, but the cultural tradition can claim no independent legitimation than through the speech which inserts it into a plurality of traditions. Each speech act, insofar as it makes a universalizing claim, can thus become the context for evaluating traditions. Thus, the performance of a post-colonial speech act constitutes the speaking person itself. Only when one understands that the best way to ensure a right important for oneself is to demand for others the right that they consider important can this new logic of association be appreciated.

5 Conclusion

The foregoing chapters have made an argument about the legitimacy of a political order. The argument has been made partly in historical terms and partly in analytical ones. This is because it is an immanent critique of the English-Canadian philosophical and political tradition. An immanent critique supposes that analytical and ethical arguments are only meaningful within a historical situation. Traditions can be altered; they can even be represented as a totality with regard to a given theme when they are confronted with another tradition, but they cannot be leapt over entirely for a supposedly self-grounding discourse of logic or ethics. The mixture of ethical argument and historical context that is operative in every political theory is made thematic here with a focus on the identity of English Canada. A political theory, and political argument more generally, operates as an attempted transformation, and ethically based will to action, within the identity of a people in the context of its relation to others.

All philosophy is 'existential' in the sense that it occurs within the middle of life. It occurs within a context, or tradition, meaning 'that which is passed on,' which contains practices, ethics, procedures, justifications, and so forth which it can never completely rationalize or master. Thus, I began my argument by sketching the outlines of this 'context,' even though I cannot do so fully (for the same reason). However, the received context of 'English-Canadian identity' and its articulation as 'English-Canadian thought' is the starting point for thinking of the question of justice. Its terminal point is an emergent universalization concerning the truth of the best political regime.

Humans are constituted such that they do not know automatically how to live, as we may presume other animals do. An answer, whether assumed or explicit, to the philosophical question 'how should humans live?' is contained within the institutions of a political order. If those who live within a given order are in accord with the dominant institutionalized answer to this question, they may live without ever posing the question clearly for themselves. To this extent, the multicultural character of contemporary societies pushes the philosophical question to the fore because it makes apparent the plurality of answers that humans have accepted. It also brings to the centre of the issue a question which did exist within the philosophical tradition but was more marginal than it can now be: what is the proper response to the fact that there is a plurality of publicly available answers to the question of what is the good life for humans?

One can regard others as merely wrong, which seems logical if one deems oneself straightforwardly right. In this case, the issue of the diversity of views about the good is subsumed under the question of what to do about those who do not see or accept the truth. Several of Plato's myths respond to this situation. If, on the other hand, there is reason to believe that there is no positive knowledge of the true political regime, then a response to the plurality of views becomes more difficult. The argument of this book with respect to diversity assumes that there is no discursive knowledge of the whole from which the question of the true political regime – the good for humans – could be definitively decided on purely rational grounds. While there may be intuitive knowledge of the whole, its political expression must enter into discourse and thus be compatible with more than one form of expression.[1] This sceptical truth is not philosophically justified here, though it is given some credibility by the historical fact of the diverse nations and identities that have existed within Canada and the threat of political uniformity that has emanated from empire, as well as a philosophical tradition that has attempted to legitimate this diversity in some form.

Philosophy's search for truth cannot replace the way of life required by a political regime, nor can it legitimate a specific regime as the only contender. No regime is 'true' in the philosophical sense. Thus, philosophy is always, in a certain sense, dependent on a way of life outside itself for its own existence. It must maintain and allow for this outside. It can neither overcome its dependence nor thoroughly legitimate an outside that would thereby cease to be outside. Philosophy is in a certain sense based on the nature/convention distinction insofar as those things taken as ultimate within a political regime are experienced and analysed by philosophy as not really ultimate, thus raising the question of what the real ultimates are, and also uncovering radically for the first time the sceptical possibility that there are really no ultimates at all. This version of the sceptical truth is all around us these days, usually under the name 'postmodernism.' But one need not embrace this Academic version of scepticism to realize the sceptical truth that there is no discursive knowledge of the whole from which the question of the true political regime could be decided. One need not deny that there is a truth of the good life but only assert that there are many ways to that truth.

The plurality of forms of expression of the truth – even if they were several forms of the same truth – means that a plurality of political regimes is compatible with the same truth. Caught in this situation, each of us must ask which form is the best, but, since each form is not total and therefore in some respect lacking, rational disagreement will occur about the best political regime. It must occur in this rational inquiry that different aspects of the best political regime are highlighted by different political traditions. The plurality and diversity of multiculturalism are for this reason basic and not merely a matter of accommodations to minorities. A politics built on this sceptical truth of philosophy must respect the incompletion derived from the plurality of approaches to the truth. In this sense, it is not a political theory but a theory of the absence of political theory, a guide to living in the community without true knowledge.

There are many ways to truth. This is a positive formulation of the sceptical truth. Thus, it is important to maintain a number of traditions within which the truth can be sought. A plurality of regimes is not only compatible with philosophy, but is demanded by it. This does not annihilate the fact that some regimes are better than others. What is the ground for this judgment? One key criterion would be a regime's maintenance of the possibility of the search for truth. This virtue of the plurality of regimes can, to a degree, legitimate a specific regime insofar as it maintains the plurality of publicly relevant ways to the truth within itself. If this is the meaning of the term 'liberal,' then it is true that the best regime will be in this sense liberal. It also implies a certain absence at the level of the highest community insofar as the question concerning the good life is not settled, but remains open to approach from many ways. The conversation about the good life constructs a friendship between traditions and thus not a finished definition but a continuing relationship. Such friendship presupposes the maintenance of viable approaches to truth, and thus the merging of these approaches cannot be complete. This incompleteness, yet acceptance, takes the political form of a treaty and is thus a practice of peace.

Notes

1: Introduction

1 Harold Innis, 'Conclusion from *The Fur Trade in Canada*,' in D. Taras, B. Rasporich, and E. Mandel, eds., *A Passion for Identity* (Toronto: Nelson Canada, 1993), 18–19.

2 Marx noted two sources of the European capitalist economy: the growth of craft workshops into manufactures due to the freeing of bonded labour and the capturing of productive processes by merchant capital. Both of these factors are internal to European development itself such that the transition from feudalism to capitalism can be captured as a history and its geographical-spatial dimension downplayed.

3 This was noted by Harold Innis in note 2/1 of *The Idea File of Harold Innis*, ed. William Christian (Toronto and Buffalo: University of Toronto Press, 1980), 6. Linda Hutcheon makes the same observation about Canadian literature in *The Canadian Postmodern* (Toronto: Oxford University Press, 1988), 3.

4 Seymour Martin Lipset, *Continental Divide: The Values and Institutions of the United States and Canada* (Toronto and Washington: C.D. Howe Institute and National Planning Association, 1989), 212.

5 Robin Mathews, *Canadian Identity* (Ottawa: Steel Rail, 1988).

6 Leslie Armour, *The Idea of Canada and the Crisis of Community* (Ottawa: Steel Rail Publishing, 1981), 109.

7 Leopoldo Zea, 'Identity: A Latin American Philosophical Problem,' in *Philosophical Forum* 20 (1988–9): 33.

8 I first appropriated the term 'universalization' in distinction from 'universal' to describe such non-subsuming identity in *Technique and Enlightenment: Limits of Instrumental Reason* (Washington: Centre for Advanced Research in Phenomenology and University Press of America, 1984), chapter 5, by

building on the work of Hannah Arendt, who herself relied on Kant's *Critique of Judgment*, which is the origin of this distinction.

2: Locality and Universalization

1 Harold Innis, 'Great Britain, the United States and Canada,' in *Essays in Canadian Economic History* (Toronto: University of Toronto Press, 1979), 395.
2 Gad Horowitz, *Canadian Labour in Politics* (Toronto: University of Toronto Press, 1972), 2.
3 Ibid., 11.
4 Ibid., 17, 10, 29.
5 Ibid., 40.
6 John Porter, *The Vertical Mosaic* (Toronto: University of Toronto Press, 1965), xiii.
7 Ibid., 92.
8 Ibid., 70.
9 John Porter, 'Ethnic Pluralism in Canada,' in Nathan Glazer and Daniel P. Moynihan, eds., *Ethnicity: Theory and Experience* (Cambridge: Harvard University Press, 1975), 297–8.
10 Graeme Patterson, *History and Communications* (Toronto: University of Toronto Press, 1990), 205.
11 Marshall McLuhan and Bruce R. Powers, *The Global Village* (New York and Oxford: Oxford University Press, 1989), 164–5.
12 Ibid., 148. Even in this descriptive context, I cannot fail to point out that the source for this reductionism is McLuhan's unjustified application of the American figure of the frontier to Canada (167) and thereby the confusion of a border with a frontier.
13 George Grant, 'Canadian Fate and Imperialism,' in *Technology and Empire* (Toronto: Anansi, 1969), 68–9.
14 Harold Innis, *The Press: A Neglected Factor in the Economic History of the Twentieth Century* (London, New York, Toronto: Oxford University Press, 1949), 5.
15 Innis, *The Idea File*, no. 2/1, 6.
16 There is a partial exception in the case of Grant insofar as he did consider French-Canadian nationalism, as he called it, but no other form of subnational particularity. See *Lament for a Nation* (Toronto and Montreal: McClelland and Stewart, 1970), chapter 6.
17 For an analysis of left-nationalism and its relation to the writings of Innis and Grant, see Ian Angus, *A Border Within: National Identity, Cultural Plurality and Wilderness* (Montreal and Kingston: McGill-Queen's University Press, 1997), 27–40.

18 Grant, *Lament for a Nation*, 85.
19 Harold Innis, 'The Strategy of Culture,' in *Changing Concepts of Time* (Toronto: University of Toronto Press, 1952), 15–16.
20 Innis, 'Great Britain, the United States and Canada,' in *Changing Concepts of Time*, 111.
21 Such a phenomenology of locality can now be seen to ground the account of the border that structured my argument in *A Border Within*. I discovered this phenomenology first through an exploration of an unfulfilled teleology in Martin Heidegger's late work. This context would unnecessarily complicate matters here and I have thus removed it. See Ian Angus, 'Place and Locality in Heidegger's Late Thought,' *Symposium* 5, no. 1 (Spring 2001): 5–23.
22 Northrop Frye, 'Conclusion to a *Literary History of Canada*,' in *The Bush Garden* (Toronto: Anansi, 1971), 220.

3: Critique of Empire

1 This account of cultural identities here rests on a phenomenological account of what Edmund Husserl called 'higher-order persons.' Such higher-order persons are self-interpreting, or, in Richard Zaner's phrase, a 'situated reflexivity.' A self is self-interpreting. The more conventional terminology of 'social groups' is misleading here, since it assumes, consistent with a pervasive ontological and/or methodological individualism, that such groups are composed of human individuals, can be dissolved into them, and therefore can be investigated as an aggregate. Edmund Husserl, *Cartesian Meditations*, trans. Dorion Cairns (The Hague: Martinus Nijhoff, 1969), 132. Cairns translates *Personalitäten höherer Ordnung* slightly misleadingly as 'higher-level personalities' insofar as, in ordinary English, it emphasizes the difference of one personality from another. 'Higher-order persons,' which I have used, corresponds more directly to Husserl's meaning of the 'person-character' of such social unities. It does follow, however, from their 'person-character' that such characters are different and thus analogous to 'personalities.' This is the condition for being able to 'reflect on (or: love, desire, hate, be disgusted with, be pleased with, remind, correct, etc.) myself.' Richard Zaner, *The Context of Self* (Athens: Ohio University Press, 1981), 151.
2 Charles Taylor, 'Impediments to a Canadian Future,' in Guy Laforest, ed., *Reconciling the Solitudes* (Montreal and Kingston: McGill-Queen's University Press, 1993), 197. See my critique of Hegelian assumptions in the politics of identity in *Primal Scenes of Communication: Communication, Consumerism and Social Movements*, (Albany: State University of New York, 2000), 64–6.
3 It would be out of place here to discuss in detail the history of the terms un-

building, destruction, deconstruction (*Abbau, Destruktion, déconstruction*) as they emerge in the history of phenomenology with Husserl, Heidegger, and Derrida. Suffice it to mention only that this problematic emerges from the 'turning-back' of thought – retrogression, *Rückgang* (Husserl), step back, *Schritt zurück* (Heidegger) – correlative to the investigation of constitution and that this turning-back is not only a movement of thought but a movement of thought that corresponds in its essence to the historical, epochal moment of its discovery. Thus, the un-building of Canada which is discussed here is a moment at which the turning-back of thought is demanded.

4 Proclamation of the Provisional Government, 8 December 1869, *Declaration of the People of Rupert's Land and the North-West*, reprinted in Prof. E.H. Oliver, ed., *The Canadian North-West: Its Early Development and Legislative Records* (Ottawa: Government Printing Bureau, 1915), 904. All subsequent quotes are from this three-page document (904–6).

5 'To the Inhabitants of the North and the North-West,' Fort Garry, 70/04/07, reprinted in Raymond Huel and George F. G. Stanley, eds., *The Collected Writings of Louis Riel*, vol. 1 (Edmonton: The University of Alberta Press, 1985), 78.

6 'Declaration of the Lillooet Tribe,' included as an appendix to Joanne Drake-Terry, *The Same as Yesterday: The Lillooet Chronicle and the Theft of Their Lands and Resources* (Lillooet: Lillooet Tribal Council, 1989), 268.

7 Ibid., 269.

8 This is the critique I make of Michael Hardt and Antonio Negri, *Empire* (Cambridge: Harvard University Press, 2000), in 'Empire, Borders, Place: A Critique of Hardt and Negri's Concept of Empire,' *Theory and Event* 7, no. 3 (2004), http://muse.jhu.edu/journals.theory_and_event/v007/7.3angus.html.

9 Stan Rowe, *Home Place: Essays on Ecology* (Edmonton: NeWest, 1990).

10 T.H. Marshall, 'Citizenship and Social Class,' in *Class, Citizenship and Social Development* (Garden City: Doubleday, 1965), 78.

11 C.B. Macpherson, 'A Political Theory of Property,' in *Democratic Theory: Essays in Retrieval* (Oxford: Clarendon Press, 1973), 131; cf. 12, 91, 134, 181.

12 Ibid., 132.

13 Nancy Fraser, 'Gender Equity and the Family Wage: A Postindustrial Thought Experiment,' in Seyla Benhabib, ed., *Democracy and Difference: Contesting the Boundaries of the Political* (Princeton: Princeton University Press, 1996).

14 See Patricia J. Mills, *Nature, Women and Psyche* (New Haven: Yale University Press, 1987).

15 Peter Kropotkin, *Fields, Factories and Workshops of Tomorrow* (New York: Harper, 1974), 26.

16 The notion of intrinsic worth, or value, is widespread in environmentalist discourse, where it is used as an opposite to instrumental value, in the way that an end is opposed to a means. It is a Kantian-derived distinction. The most influential version is probably by Arne Naess, *Ecology, Community and Lifestyle*, trans. David Rothenberg (Cambridge: Cambridge University Press, 1989).

17 The issue of unpaid work is a persistent, if not front-and-centre, theme in both environmental and feminist discourses. For discussions which connect them, see Vandana Shiva, *Staying Alive: Women, Ecology and Development* (London: Zed Books, 1988), and André Gorz, *Capitalism, Socialism, Ecology*, trans. Chris Turner (London and New York: Verso, 1994).

18 See, for example, Ivan Illich, *Shadow Work* (Boston and London: Marion Boyars, 1981); Alejandro Portes, Manuel Castells, and Lauren A. Benton, *The Informal Economy* (Baltimore and London: Johns Hopkins University Press, 1989); and Claus Offe and Rolf G. Heinze, *Beyond Employment*, trans. Alan Braley (Cambridge: Polity Press, 1992).

19 I hope that this phrasing avoids a possible misunderstanding of the perspective that I am advocating. Unwaged labour has often been, for that very reason, a source of dependence and exploitation, and therefore, in many cases, access to wage labour has been a liberating experience. Similarly, giving environmental goods a price would give them some standing in the market. Nevertheless, I am arguing that the real locus of wealth is in subsistence and that the transformation of work into wage labour has intrinsic limitations.

20 Carolyn Merchant, for example, describes eco-feminism as a critique of the market economy that suggests 'partnership,' both with other humans and with nature, as an alternative ethic. See *Radical Ecology: The Search for a Livable World* (London and New York: Routledge, 1992), 183–8. Other writers have suggested an ethic of care. Cf. William Leiss, *Under Technology's Thumb* (Montreal and Kingston: McGill-Queen's University Press, 1990), chapter 13. Others still have suggested 'respect.' Cf. Ian Angus, *A Border Within*, 160–70. The current point is that all of these alternatives depend upon a displacement of the market from its monopoly of the social representation of value.

21 Karl Polanyi, *The Great Transformation* (Boston: Beacon Press, 1971).

22 Understanding contemporary capitalist society as a community–market tension in this way, as opposed to the Marxist 'class contradiction,' has the advantage of not counterposing an earlier, supposedly universalist movement to later 'identity politics.' It would be too much to say that there has been no change here, but the present analysis underlines the particular origins of all movements and the universalizing performed in attaining hege-

mony in a way that undercuts those who would regard the difference as fundamental. For an example of the latter polarization, which prevails both among identity theorists and class theorists, see Nancy Fraser, 'From Redistribution to Recognition? Dilemmas of Justice in a "Postsocialist" Age,' in *Justice Interruptus: Critical Reflections on the 'Postsocialist' Condition* (New York and London: Routledge, 1997).

23 I will mention some possibilities, but their purpose is simply illustration of a perspective, not the setting out of strategic goals. Community control of investment through credit unions, if possible combined with legislation forcing banks toward the devolution of investment decisions, would be a component. Diverse forms of ownership of local enterprises are also important. Social ownership through municipal and community boards, worker control, small business, and many other forms can all promote a diverse and sustainable local economy. Flexibility in the work day, including job sharing and part-time jobs with full benefits, would allow a dedication of an increasing share of one's time to subsistence – rather than being faced with a 'choice' between full-time wage labour or unemployment.

24 This perspective is often called 'community economic development.' See, for example, Burt Galaway and Joe Hudson, eds., *Community Economic Development: Perspectives on Research and Policy* (Toronto: Thompson, 1994), and David P. Ross and Peter J. Usher, *From the Roots Up: Economic Development as if Community Mattered* (Toronto: James Lorimer, 1986).

25 A global market is, in a certain sense, still compatible with the perspective outlined here. But it should be a market in non-necessities, a market from which subsistence is gradually withdrawn. Another possibility is that 'fair trade' principles could be established between equal regions and nations. For such equality to be viable, however, it would seem to require the possibility of opting out, which would require that this option be a practical possibility. Thus, I conclude that subsistence should be, to the greatest possible extent, satisfied in a non-market fashion. This is an orienting perspective, one must recall, not a plan. Also relevant here is that a 'necessity' would be so defined by political deliberations and would become debatable as the price of 'independence.' Thus, while 'independence' does not mean 'isolation,' it does seem to imply the practical possibility of separation – even if the price is high and only contemplated in the extreme case.

4: The Principle of Association

1 John Locke, *A Letter Concerning Toleration* (Englewood Cliffs: Prentice Hall, 1950), 17, 20.

2 Ibid., 16, 31.
3 Ibid., 34.
4 Ibid., 52.
5 W.B. Gallie, 'Essentially Contested Concepts,' in *Proceedings of the Aristotelian Society*, vol. 56 (London: Harrison and Sons, 1956).
6 Hannah Arendt, 'The Crisis in Culture,' in *Between Past and Future* (New York: The Viking Press, 1961), 221.
7 Immanuel Kant, *Critique of Judgment*, trans. J.H. Bernard (New York: Collier Macmillan, 1974), 182–6.
8 I use the common term 'reflexive,' based on the image of reflection in water or a mirror, here even though it is, strictly speaking, incorrect due to the basis of the term in the objectification of the world in modernity. The 'step back' (Heidegger) as a continuation of the 'transcendental reduction' (Husserl) is the correct lineage here of the concept of thought intended, in distinction to the Hegelian origin of the term 'reflection.' See Martin Heidegger, 'Overcoming Metaphysics' in *The End of Philosophy*, trans. Joan Stambaugh (New York: Harper and Row, 1973), 97ff. The difference between reflection and the step back as descriptions of the consciousness attained by historical articulation refers to the issue of an 'essentially contested concept' (Gallie) and 'judgment' (Arendt): it is a form of thought which is not directed to making valid conclusions based upon assumed premises but toward inquiring about the valid, or proper, starting points from which arguments in the normal sense derive. It is a 'turning-back' of the normal direction of thought rather than a second reflection on normal thought from a higher perspective.
9 A drastically new interpretation could only be introduced by unsettling the common presuppositions of such settled historical interpretations. Such an unsettling is the meaning of the operation of deconstruction and indicates its relationship to historical hermeneutics. It is this operation that I am trying to perform on the third interpretation of Canadian Federalism. It is rooted in the phenomenological 'turning-back,' or 'step back.'
10 Donald Creighton, 'The Myth of Biculturalism,' in *Towards the Discovery of Canada* (Toronto: Macmillan, 1972), 267.
11 James Tully, *Strange Multiplicity: Constitutionalism in an Age of Diversity* (Cambridge: Cambridge University Press, 1995), 140.
12 Samuel LaSelva, *The Moral Foundations of Canadian Federalism* (Montreal and Kingston: McGill-Queen's University Press, 1966), 39.
13 Tully, *Strange Multiplicity*, 172.
14 Samuel LaSelva, *Moral Foundations*, 29. But it is not sufficiently clear theoretically to describe Federalists of this third stripe as, first, neither universalists

nor particularists and, second, as 'accommodating' both/and. He also refers to it in an unsatisfactory way as a 'middle ground,' indicating a failure to think through the implications of this political history at a theoretical level. *Moral Foundations*, 188.

15 J.M.S. Careless, '"Limited Identities" in Canada,' in *Careless at Work* (Toronto: Dundurn, 1990), 284.

16 It is possible that the logic of inclusion, which promotes the creation of ever-larger unities through the recognition and incorporation of particularities, may have an inherent limit. While it can always aspire to a one-higher unity, as it were, it is possible that the 'final' unity could not be totally inclusive. If it is true that a socio-cultural unity is necessarily constituted through reference to its outside, then a singular unity of all humanity is not possible. Or, it may be possible only on the condition that humanity as a whole opposes itself to its outside – either nature or God – which then rebounds inside to repress the natural substratum of humanity. However, even if this is so, it does not constitute a reason to abandon the logic of inclusion as such.

17 See, for example, Frank Cunningham, 'Democracy and Three-Nation Asymmetry,' *Canadian Forum* (December 1992): 18–9; Will Kymlicka, *Finding Our Way* (Toronto: Oxford University Press, 1998), 160–4; and Philip Resnick, *Thinking English Canada* (Toronto: Stoddart, 1994), chapter 10.

18 This is not to say that the principle of association has no implications for, or influence on, the internal constitution of groups. As I have indicated briefly in the preceding paragraph, communities take a different, more open form when they exist within a field of communities. This is the reason why, to take one example, contemporary multiculturalism is not simply a defence of traditionalism.

19 Pierre-Joseph Proudhon, *The Federal Principle* (1863), excerpted in *Selected Writings of Pierre-Joseph Proudhon* (Garden City: Anchor Books, 1969), 106–7.

20 Joseph Gosnell, 'Speech to the British Columbia Legislature, December 2, 1998,' in *BC Studies* 120 (Winter 1998–9): 9.

21 Jeremy Brecher, Tim Costello, and Brendan Smith, *Globalization from Below: The Power of Solidarity* (Cambridge: South End Press, 2000), 110.

22 Note however that a First Nations identity does pose an issue of whether it can be reconciled with Canadian national identity as does, to a lesser extent, a Québécois identity. Why is this so? Because these identities remain 'outside' the national identity due to the unameliorated nature of their violent inclusion. An ethnic identity becomes an ethnic identity precisely because it leaves no remainder 'outside' the national. This issue can only be resolved through understanding the constitution of a 'minority bar,' as I will argue later in this chapter.

23 J.L. Austin, *How to Do Things with Words* (Cambridge: Harvard University Press, 1975), 6.
24 See David Konstan, *Friendship in the Classical World* (Cambridge: Cambridge University Press, 1997), 83ff.
25 Noel Dyck, *What Is the Indian Problem?* (St John's: Institute for Social and Economic Research, 1991), 24.

5: Conclusion

1 This issue takes the form in the history of philosophy of an evaluation of the superiority of Socrates' inconclusiveness over Plato's theory of the whole. My version of the defence of Socrates is to be found in 'Socrates and the Critique of Metaphysics,' *The European Legacy* 10, no. 4 (2005): 299–314.

Index